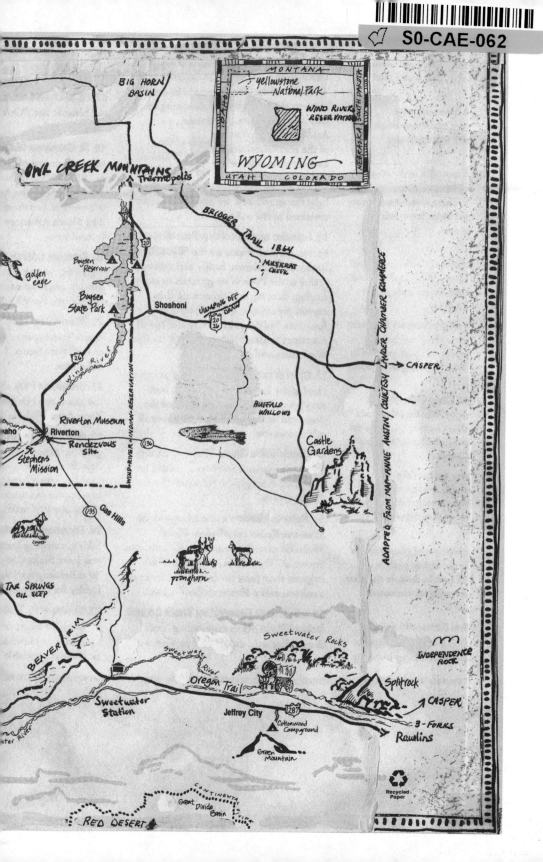

BIG HORN BASIN

OWL CREEK MOUNTAINS

Thermopolis

MONTANA
Yellowstone National Park
WIND RIVER RESERVATION

WYOMING

UTAH   COLORADO

NEBRASKA
SOUTH DAKOTA

BRIDGER TRAIL 1864

MUSKRAT CREEK

golden eagle

Boysen Reservoir

Boysen State Park

Shoshoni

JUMPING OFF DRAW

20
26

20

26

CASPER

BUFFALO WALLOWS

Wind River

Riverton Museum

Riverton

Rendezvous Site

St. Stephens Mission

aho

WINDRIVER INDIAN RESERVATION

136

Castle Gardens

ADAPTED FROM MAP: ANNE AUSTIN / COURTESY LANDER CHAMBER COMMERCE

135

Gas Hills

coyote

TAR SPRINGS OIL SEEP

pronghorn

BEAVER RIM

Sweetwater Rocks

INDEPENDENCE ROCK

Sweetwater River

Oregon Trail

Sweetwater Station

Jeffrey City

287

Cottonwood Campground

Splitrock

CASPER

3-FORKS

Rawlins

ter River

Green Mountain

CONTINENTAL

Great Divide Basin

DIVIDE

RED DESERT

Recycled Paper

Walk Softly, This is God's Country

Sixty-Six Years on the Wind River Indian Reservation

compiled from the letters and journals of
The Rev. John Roberts
1883-1949

Elinor R. Markley
and
Beatrice Crofts

Contents

Acknowledgments
Introduction
Foreword

Part 1 — The Work

Chapter 1:   The Blizzard 7

Chapter 2:   Co-Inhabitants of the Reservation 10

Chapter 3:   Early Living conditions and Traditions 22

Chapter 4:   Shoshone Ministry—Shoshone Friends 32

Chapter 5:   Early Services on the Reservation 40

Chapter 6:   Medicine Men and Superstitions 50

Chapter 7:   The Sundance 53

Chapter 8:   Early Education—Roberts' Mission 59

Chapter 9:   School Life 76

Chapter 10:   Arapahoe Ministry; Arapahoe Friends 83

Chapter 11:   St. Michael's — The Arapahoe Episcopal Mission 98

Chapter 12:   Summing up the Reservation Work 102

Chapter 13   On the Road — Ministry to the White Settlements 105

Part 2 — Washakie, Sacajawea and Laura Roberts

Chapter 1   Washakie 116

Chapter 2   Sacajawea 131

Chapter 3   Sherman Coolidge 141

Chapter 4   Laura Roberts 148

Conclusion   158

Epilogue   160

Appendix #1 167

Appendix #2 172

Acknowledgments 195

Introduction

by Beatrice Crofts

In 1883 my grandfather, Rev. John Roberts, came to what is now called the Wind River Indian Reservation of central Wyoming. There he spent the rest of his life, working as both missionary and educator among the Shoshone, Arapahoe and early settlers until his death in 1949.

Highly educated himself, Rev. Roberts was afraid that much of this era, so critical to those Indians making the difficult transitions of early reservation life, would be lost or forgotten. To preserve this, John Roberts wrote down stories and legends as well as accounts of events and of the many characters he came to know and love in the course of his work. He made copies of his correspondence and of letters written to him concerning living conditions and official church and government policies.

Unlike many of his colleagues, Roberts was concerned with helping the Indians retain their cultural identity and language while at the same time learning to cope with the demands of white society. Fluent, as was the entire family, in both Shoshone and Arapahoe, he not only translated hymns and liturgy but also compiled the first known lists of Shoshone and Arapahoe vocabulary along with pronunciation keys. Examples of these are included in the appendix of this book. The result of this careful gathering and preserving is a rich historical legacy about a little known period of Wyoming history.

My mother, Elinor Roberts Markley, was born on the Reservation along with sisters Gwen, Marion and Gladys, and her brother Dr. Edward Roberts. After graduating from California State Teacher's College at San Jose, Elinor returned to the Reservation and taught at the Wind River Indian Agency for a few years. She married Charles Markley, who had graduated from business college in Kansas City and had come to the Reservation as the bookkeeper for the James Moore Trading Company at Fort Washakie. In about 1932 Elinor taught school again, this time at the Fort Washakie District School.

After retiring around 1957, Elinor made it her mission to put much of her father's material into book form. She arranged and typed all of Grandfather's papers before attempting to incorporate them into the

Elinor Roberts Markley — College Graduation, California State Teacher's College San Jose, CA.
(From Author's Collection)

narrative of her own memoirs.[1] This was a laborious task. Grandfather Roberts wrote in old English script; at times it was barely legible and through the years the ink had faded, making the task of deciphering his words even more difficult. Because times were hard and writing materials scarce, he often covered a sheet and then turned it sideways and continued writing up the edge of the paper.

The result of my mother's efforts, a very rough draft of this present book subtitled *Memoirs of Sixty-six Years on an Indian Reservation*, was placed for safe keeping in the Western History Archives at the University of Wyoming along with some of my grandfather's papers. Dr. Sharon Kahin came across this manuscript in its original form in the course of research undertaken for the *Valley of Three Worlds* project which was sponsored by Central Wyoming College in 1986-1987 and funded by a grant from the National Endowment for the Humanities. It was she who encouraged me to prepare my mother's work for publication. With the help of Dr. Kahin, I have edited these memoirs and annotated them with personal memories and reminiscences from my own Reservation childhood.

Several excerpts from Elinor's original manuscript have been published from time to time, both with and without the family's permission. While there is no doubt that John Roberts' papers and my mother's manuscript are the original sources of these borrowings, these sources have not always been acknowledged. I believe it is now time for this material to be presented all in one piece, as it was originally conceived. In 1990 a generous grant to the Dubois Museum from the Wyoming Council for the Humanities to research and prepare important historical manuscripts as part of its Centennial Project made this version possible. Dr. Guy Lytle of the University of the South, Sewanee, Tennessee, gave a generous donation on behalf of the Episcopal Historical Society in order to encourage this project.

---

[1] *I believe my mother started collecting this material shortly after my grandfather died in 1949 and wrote the main part of her memoirs in the late 50's.*

Foreword

By Elinor Roberts Markley

John Roberts was born March 31, 1853, of Welsh parents at Llewllyd, a country place about two miles east of Rhuddlan, North Wales. He attended Welsh grammar schools and in 1876 graduated with a B.A. from St. David's, Lampeter, a college affiliated with Oxford University. In 1878 he was ordained to the Deaconate by the Rt. Rev. George Augustus Selwyn in Lichfield Cathedral.

For a short time Roberts was appointed curate at Dawley Magna in Shropshire. From there he went to the Bahama Islands, British West Indies. At Nassau he was ordained to the priesthood by the Rt. Rev. Francis Cramer Roberts and placed in charge of St. Matthew's Cathedral. In addition to his duties at the Nassau cathedral, Roberts assisted the bishop in his work among the colored people, especially those in the leper colonies on some of the outer-islands.

Arduous as this work was, it was not what John Roberts had envisioned when he was ordained; his parishioners in the West Indies were already Christians and he was seeking a greater challenge. After two years Roberts sailed again, this time to New York where he applied for the Mission he had always wanted — a ministry among the American Indians. In New York City, Roberts asked the Bishop of Wyoming and Colorado, the Rev. John F. Spalding, for "missionary work in your most difficult field." The answer came: "We have it — the Shoshone and Bannock Indian Agency on the Shoshone Indian Reservation, Wyoming Territory."

As a first step, Bishop Spalding sent John Roberts to Greeley, Colorado and then on to Pueblo to work among the coal miners. At Pueblo, Roberts became rector of Trinity Church and in 1882 established the Trinity Mission in South Pueblo. While in Colorado, an epidemic of smallpox broke out. As long as it lasted Roberts lived and worked, quarantined in the Pueblo hospital, doing what he could for the patients. He had only one complaint during that time — the convalescent young ladies would, without his permission, borrow his extra clothes and so disguised, head for town!

Then on February 1, 1883, Roberts left Pueblo by train and traveled via Cheyenne to his new destination – Green River, Wyoming.

John Roberts, Photo circa 1874
Taken in Bahama Islands, British West Indies
Photos from Author's Collection

Chapter 1

The Blizzard

The regular stagecoach, carrying passengers and mail, did not leave Green River, Wyoming, for the Shoshone and Bannock Indian Agency on the second day of February, 1883, because of the great blizzard. The agency was 150 miles away, and the trip, even in favorable weather, was hazardous. Surely no passenger would think of undertaking it in such a storm.

But the mail must go through! Four horses were harnessed to a big wooden, dry-goods box on runners. Hay was spread on the floor of the

Freight, mail and passenger sled similar to the one used by Roberts in 1883
Photo taken at South Pass

box, and a plank was placed across the open wagon, resting on the two sides near the front. Though the plank qualified as a seat, the floor proved to be a better one as it afforded some slight shelter to the travelers from the high, icy winds and blowing snow.

The driver was almost ready to start when he noticed a young man carrying a small traveling bag standing near the sled, his dog waiting by his side. The young man told the driver his name was John Roberts and that he wished to go to the Indian Reservation as soon as possible.

"You're just a-bustin' to go along, ain't you!" exclaimed the driver. "Well, come ahead. Got you a coat? That ain't no coat, get you an extry one off'n m'bed."

Along the road between Green River and the Reservation, were stage stations about 15 or 20 miles apart where a change of horses and sometimes a change of drivers was made. With the greatest anticipation, travelers would see the cabins in the distance ahead of them, where a meal was available. After dark, in clear weather, how cheering it was to everyone in the coach to see the lighted windows of the station shining, even two or three miles away. Some of these stations were named Separation Flats (called Myers at the time), Alkali, Big Sandy, Little Sandy, Dry Sandy, South Pass (by-passing Pacific Springs), Ed Young's, Lander and Shoshone Agency.

The storm which struck the divide the last day of January covered the whole area with deep snow and mountainous drifts hid the roads. Several people, caught in the storm and unable to find their way to shelter, were frozen to death or died some time afterward as a result of exposure to the intense cold. At Dry Sandy, the Rev. John Roberts officiated at the burial service of George Rider, a stage driver who had been frozen to death in the first days of the storm while attempting to get the mail through. The record reads: "Frozen while carrying the mail, buried in the snow at Dry Sandy, whence the body was subsequently removed."

At the same station, there was an eighteen year old girl, Maggie Sherlock, who was very ill. She was suffering from extreme exposure, and later died. She had been caught in the storm while on her way to school in Salt Lake City. The young clergyman, anxious to help the patient and her family, could do so only indirectly by chopping wood the whole day and keeping the little station comfortable.

William B. Clark[2] also perished in the storm; his body was found a month later. The Rev. John Roberts officiated at his funeral on March 4th. Clark was buried at the Lander Cemetery.

This trip, made by the two travelers in the dry-goods box on runners, took eight days instead of the usual 36-hour trip made by the regular stage. When asked by a friend how he survived the cold, Mr. Roberts answered, "It was very cold but I managed to keep from freezing by

---

[2] *There are still relatives of Maggie Sherlock and William Clark living in this area. Georgia Bower is the granddaughter of William Clark.*

shoveling snow ahead of the team much of the way from Green River to the Shoshone Indian Agency."

When the two finally arrived at their destination on February 10, 1883, the government thermometer at Fort Washakie, a mile from the agency, registered sixty degrees below zero. As the sled went over the last hill, its two passengers saw what appeared to be a valley filled with Japanese lanterns. These lanterns were really many teepees lighted by a sagebrush fire burning in each. The Shoshones and Arapahoes had moved their camps near the agency where rations of food and clothing would be issued to them the next day.

The young missionary was pleasantly surprised to find anything like the trader's store and post office into which he hurried to get warm. With a big fire roaring in the stove, there seemed to be friendliness with the warmth. It was almost luxurious after coming so many desolate miles and passing lonely stage stations. As he stepped inside the store, he heard a man say, "The preacher's come."

Then the answer, "That's no preacher, he's got him a dog!"

That night, quilts and a borrowed buffalo robe spread on two benches placed together in the cabin of a kind stranger were his first bed and home on the Wind River Indian Reservation.

Church of the Holy Sts John, Shoshone Mission

Chapter 2

Co-Inhabitants of the Reservation

When Mr. Roberts arrived at his new field of work, Wyoming was still a virgin country; civilization had scarcely reached its borders. The only means of travel from the terminal of the Union Pacific railroad, at Rawlins was the "prairie schooner." For the more fortunate, perhaps the stagecoach was used. The route Mr. Roberts was obliged to take from Green River to the Shoshone Agency was over mountains, prairies and across a wilderness covered with snow, the deepest in years.

Had the clergyman been able to make the trip during a more favorable season, he would have seen a glorious country. Wide stretches of prairie have a beauty of their own, especially in the early spring when the wild flowers grow profusely. There were almost no fences, roads or bridges. If the usual river crossings were too deep for a team to ford, a series of calls or a gun shot usually alerted some man on the river who made a few dollars by running a ferry. If the end of the day found a traveler too far from his destination, he was, however, quite sure of a welcome with food and a bed at a hospitable ranch home.

At this time, the Shoshone and Arapahoe tribes were co-inhabiting the Wind River Reservation. The Reservation was first known as the Shoshone and Bannock Reservation, then the Shoshone Indian Reservation, and now it is known as the Wind River Indian Reservation. The original military post, Camp Brown, was moved near the banks of the Little Wind River in 1871. This was all prairie land. In 1879, on March 24, Post teams arrived from the railroad bringing in trees from Utah. Irrigation ditches were dug. In January, 1879, the name was changed from Camp Brown to Fort Washakie by Order of the War Department in honor of the celebrated Chief of the Shoshones. Fort Washakie was a very important place to all of us who made our home on this Reservation. It was the hub of all activity for Indians and Whites when my grandfather arrived there in 1883. It was also the center of my world, having lived there most of my life until I was married. By the Treaty of 1868, Chief Washakie succeeded in obtaining the Wind River Valley as a home for the Shoshones. The original Reservation was established by the Fort Bridger Treaty of 1863. Some time during October 1877, Dr. James Irwin, the Indian agent, directed

Weasaw, an early-day Shoshone man

by the United States Indian Department, obtained the Chief's unwilling consent to place the northern band of Arapahoes on the Shoshone Reservation for the winter of 1877-1878. At that time the government promised to find a separate reservation for the Arapahoes in the near future. Such a promise was never fulfilled and the Arapahoes never moved. Many years later the Shoshones were compensated for the land occupied by the Arapahoe tribe.

In the 1930's, my family's dream was the same as that of the Shoshone people. Everyone believed that "When the Tunnison money came..." we would all have enough. There was always great excitement on the Reservation if word was spread that Mr. Tunnison was coming. The "Tunnison money" was the payment this eastern lawyer, George Tunnison, was going to get from the United States. It was payment for land given by the government to the Arapahoe Indians, land that had already been given to the Shoshone people.

My parents' great hope was that with this money all of the Shoshones would soon have adequate food, clothing, shelter and a few of the very bare necessities of life; that, finally being able to pay for these things, they would regain their pride. For years my father had run a store on the Reservation. But for him it was impossible to run a grocery store among a starving people, so he gave groceries away as long as he could. At that time the Indians had no buffalo hides to trade; in fact they had very little of anything to trade for food, and there were few game animals left in the country.

At last the great day did arrive. The lawyer, Mr. Tunnison, won the case and in April, 1938, the Shoshone people were awarded four million, four hundred eight thousand, four hundred forty-four dollars ($4,408,444). This was a wonderful day on the Reservation. For the first time the Shoshones had money, their own money, with which to buy a few things. As I look back on this time, this day changed many things on the Reservation. I don't ever remember seeing Tunnison, but I do know that he became a millionaire overnight when the case was settled in court. He was given the same amount of money in the settlement as was awarded to the Indians. He became a millionaire, and the Indians became customers for all the products of the White world.

When Rev. Roberts first came there, the Indians neither spoke nor understood English. After some time and after many embarrassing mistakes, he was able to converse with both the Shoshones and Arapahoes in their own languages and in the common sign language. But there were obstacles and hardships to be endured and overcome, more vital than the barrier of the languages, if one were to survive. There was the intense cold of winter from which there was extremely inadequate shelter. In many camps, besides cold, there was hunger, illness and often, fear. The opposition of the medicine men had to be faced. The Indians lived in dread of the power of the medicine men, their minds burdened with many distressing superstitions and cruel beliefs. There was isolation. Sometimes the stagecoach with its precious mail from the outside world didn't get in. Often the freight teams with supplies were many days late.

Almost no missionary work had been done among the Indians on the Wind River Reservation before 1883[3]. Should an old Indian of either tribe be in a reminiscent mood, he could tell many a grim tale of disaster and death due to tribal hatred.

~~~

Our Indians in Wyoming were not cultivators of the ground until about 50 years ago. They have no traditions concerning the pumpkin or the squash. The Arapahoes have a sacred ear of corn which they claim was presented to the first Arapahoe by the Creator, the Unknown On High, "seven old men ago," (i.e. 80 or 90 x 7 ago), but they did not plant corn or other grain until they came on this Reservation in 1878. Both tribes subsisted in times past almost entirely on game, dried berries, roots and seeds which they made into a thick gruel.

The Shoshones are a naturally friendly and good natured people. They claim they alone are true Indians. They may be right because their native customs, superstitions and traditions and even appearance were strikingly similar to those of the Hindus. They believed their original home was in the land beyond the setting sun where they went after death, where they would be made over. They believed in the transmigration of souls.

The Shoshones are undoubtedly a very ancient people. In their ways they are quite close to nature and in some things are uncannily perceptive. Long before the fact was discovered by scientists, they attributed the cause of Rocky Mountain fever to the gopher.[4] One day in conversation

---

[3] *St. Stephens Catholic Mission began ministering to the Araphoe on the Eastern portion about 1884.*

[4] *Prairie dogs or gophers harbor ticks which are known to carry this disease.*

with Rev. John Roberts, his friend Wit-to-gan, a Shoshone, complained that the government farmer, Mr. F. G. Burnett, insisted that he irrigate his wheat field so that he would have plenty of flour for bread for his family. Mr. Roberts asked him, "What do you care if that gopher comes out of his flooded burrow and looks at you?" "I will die!" the Shoshone replied. Then Mr. Roberts asked Wit-to-gan, "You don't believe that, do you?" He answered, "Of course I do. I will die." Some of the old Indians used to say that if a dead gopher were found near their teepee, there surely would be mountain fever, as tick fever was called at that time in the camp. Mr. Roberts and others had noticed that where there were gopher mounds, the dreaded fever was more prevalent. The fear of these small animals was so strong among the Indians that Mr. Roberts sent the story to the Smithsonian Institution. As a result, some representatives from the Institution came to the Shoshone Reservation to talk with Mr. Roberts and with many of the Indians. They then went to Montana where the fever was very severe. A wonderful immunization against the disease was the result.

Legend also speaks of *schtheol*,[5] a medicinal substance made from salmon in Idaho which the Shoshones used in treatment of rheumatism.

The word "Shoshone" is derived from two words, "shaunt" meaning much and "shonip" meaning grass. It was formerly the custom of these people to camp where grass for their wigwams was plentiful. The tribe is a branch of the great Snake family of North American Indians embracing the Eastern and Western Shoshones, the Bannocks, Utes, Comanches, Kiowas, Paiutes and several of the small tribes of the Pacific coast.

The Shoshones are not all proud of the name or sign "snake." I believe that both are applied to them by others rather than claimed by themselves. The sign for Bannock (Ban-ni-te) is made by holding the open left hand, palm down, in front of and about twelve inches from the left side of the chest and then touching the middle of the palm of the left hand with the tip of the first finger of the right hand with the rest of the hand closed. The Shoshones and Bannocks have little to say of their relationship but they have always been friends and allies.

The Shoshones are what may be termed "mountain Indians" differing physically and mentally from the so-called "plains Indians." The Snake Indians on the Wind River Reservation were divided into three clans: the Duke-a-dika, Beef Eaters; the Seep-a-dika, Sheep Eaters; and the Nima-so-g-meer, Pedestrians.

---

[5] *We have not been able to identify Schtheol, the substance mentioned above.*

An Early Arapahoe Photo (thought to be taken in London)

The last were the most numerous but least influential. Their progenitor was the great coyote whom they called the "father of lies." At first they had no country until a chickadee discovered the earth. Because of the insolence of Coyote in using ventriloquism to address the Creator (Dam Newinip), he brought the curse of death upon his descendants.

According to their own story, the Shoshones separated from the Comanches a little more than a century ago. The Shoshones claim that at that time their clan was the more numerous. As to the Indian himself, he has little to say of his past history, especially when he feels that information is sought. At times, if he knows he is talking to friends, he will open his heart. But these intervals are rare and only those men who have lived long among them are in possession of the true knowledge of the Indian history of the country.

The Arapahoe too have their sacred history. A short time after Mr. Roberts came to the Reservation, the Arapahoes went on their annual buffalo hunt to the wild region where the city of Casper now stands, a distance of some 150 miles from the Agency. The custodian of the Arapahoes' Sacred Pipe, who was then an old man, had not joined the tribal hunt but had established a winter camp not far from Fort Washakie. One night Mr. Roberts' cabin door opened and the venerable custodian of the Sacred Pipe came to take refuge from an attack of hostile Indians. When it grew late, Mr. Roberts pointed to some blankets. In the morning the old Arapahoe left, still carrying the pipe wrapped in its pelts and skins. Not a word had been spoken.

At another time of hostile uprising, this Sacred Pipe was entrusted entirely to Mr. Roberts and he was shown the pipe. At that time, he was the first and only White man to be so honored.

The Sacred Pipe was of great historical significance. It had been handed to an Arapahoe at the time of the creation of the world as a token of the creator's everlasting promise to care for and protect the Arapahoes from generation to generation. Arapahoes believed that when they died those who gazed upon the Sacred Pipe would be carried safely to "Ha-ya-in," their home. For that reason The Arapahoes called it the "Chariot of God, Hodde Je-van-e-au-thau." Another name was "Si-eja" because it was flat in form. It would take hours to tell all the history of the pipe; it led the Arapahoes for many generations. The pipe was so sacred that at all times it was borne by the custodian on foot. It was passed down from generation to generation with solemn ceremony. The old men used to tell of the great sacrifice made once in every generation when all the men of the tribe offered themselves, with bowed heads, before the custodian of the pipe. One of them was chosen by him to die for the tribe.

Neither the Arapahoes nor the Shoshones seem to have any knowledge concerning the hieroglyphics (petroglyphs) found in Fremont county. To these Indians they seem to be pre-historic. One old Shoshone had his explanation, but it was founded upon very uncertain tradition. He says: "They are the work of Bo-he, a very beneficent mountain demon in human shape, who in former times would descend at night to warn Shoshones camped near the rocks of future dangers from their enemies. Waking at night, these hunters would hear mysterious tapping on a nearby rock. Bo-he, though invisible, would converse with them telling them how to guard against their enemies. He would return to the mountain passes before dawn. The hunters would find sharp flint with which the tracings had been made near the inscribed rock. They would carry these with them on their persons as talismans."

~~~

The last serious trouble involving the two tribes occurred in 1907 over the signing of the treaty by which that portion of the Reservation north of the Big Wind River (a little less than one and a half million acres) was thrown open to settlement. Eight hundred thousand acres were left to be allotted to the Indians in Severalty.[6] The proceeds of the sale exceeded one million dollars. This sum was to be used to purchase livestock for the Indians, to construct irrigation ditches, and to form a general welfare fund, which the Indians in council would direct and the Secretary of the Interior approve.[7] The policy of the Department was to place each family on a good allotment of 160 acres of farming land under irrigation. As a tribe, the Shoshones as well as the Arapahoes were willing to sign the

---

[6] *Severalty or individual ownership led to difficulties in later years as numerous descendants owning the same land caused problems of inheritance.*

[7] *Wild game was scarce when Grandpapa came to the Reservation. An excerpt from* The Annual Report of the Commissioner of Indian Affairs to the Secretary of the Interior for the Year 1885, *(Washington Government Printing Office, page 212) states:*

Not over ten buffalo robes have been brought in this year, showing the animal is almost extinct, and that the Indian can no longer look to the buffalo as a source of supply. Elk are becoming scarce and deer and antelope can only be found after miles of hard travel and weary day's hunt. There is no market for buckskin, and elk hide will not bring over 50 cents per pound in the Eastern market.

In the year 1882 the Indians sold 2,400 buffalo robes; in 1883, 1,500; in 1884, 500; and in 1885, 10. In 1883 the Indians sold 4,500 pounds of deer and elk; in 1884, 6,000 pounds; and in 1885, 7,000 pounds, worth 35 cents per pound at the present time. They brought in about eight hundred pounds of beaver, worth $1.50 per pound, and other furs to the amount of $500.

---

treaty but there was a dissatisfied clique which objected to the agreement, refused to sign and spoke strongly against it.

In January of the same year there was a brutal murder caused by this dissension, and the greatest apprehension was felt by the White people. Even the Indians carried arms and avoided going out after dark. Some stood guard over their homes all night.

The Rev. John Roberts, returning home from holding a service at Milford, saw what he thought might be an ambush in the hills ahead of him — four posted Indians who on signal began to close in on him. He turned his team around and went back to Milford. All the circumstances taken together caused him considerable uneasiness when he remembered that Mrs. Roberts was alone at the Mission. At Milford, he at once telegraphed to the commanding officer, Major Sands at Fort Washakie, for an escort to take her down to the fort. Mr. Roberts returned to the Mission the next day accompanied, at the insistence of Major Sands, by a detail of soldiers. He said afterwards that had he known less of the past records of some of the "fanatics" he would not have felt such keen anxiety over the whole affair. He had been in several uprisings during his residence on the Reservation but he had not been in the least apprehensive of any danger until this last most unfortunate occurrence.[8]

For a time, it seemed that there would be no treaty. Yellow Calf, a leader among the Arapahoes, and supported by the Rev. Sherman Coolidge and a strong following of Rev. John Roberts' former school boys, rose up

---

[8] *The following correspondence between my grandfather and Bishop Funsten, the Hon. F. Chatterton and my mother, Nellie, throws some light on the situation and concern generated by this incident.*

My dear Bishop [Funsten],

I am afraid my letter of yesterday may have caused you some anxiety but there is no reason for any whatever. As I said, both tribes, the Arapahoes just as much as the Shoshones, are true friends of mine. The disaffected ones are only a clique and know the money, $50.00 each, in payment for the land, has come and those who had refused their allotments on the ceded *portion are assured that they can get other allotments on the Diminished Reservation; everything will go as usual. Mr. Wadsworth, who has been absent, came in today in the post ambulance. He was very uneasy and did not bring his family. So has Mr. Burnett and others here, been uneasy since poor Mr. Terry, the Shoshone Councilman and spokesman for the Treaty signers, was so brutally and stealthily murdered. The disaffected ones among the lower Arapahoes, whom I especially feared, on account of the Treaty, disclaim all sinister purposes whatever. On my return from a funeral at Milford, I saw in the hills before me what might have been a trap, four posted Indians, who at a signal, began to close in on me. I turned the buggy around and returned. On their retirement I feared for Mrs. Roberts and the children who were alone at the Mission. And remembering from what had been intimated to me...I feared for the safety of my family. I telegraphed to Fort Washakie to ask that Mrs. Roberts and the children be taken down to the Fort. I went back to Lander, intending to return the next day, but the commanding officer telegraphed that he would send an escort for me. I declined but he insisted. I do not like to refuse him and the show of force has had a very good effect on unruly ones, though I should have preferred to have come back alone. I do not run any unnecessary risk, and I feel sure the danger, if there was any, has passed by...Everything is going on quietly, both Miss Maude Lee and Miss Doughty are here with the girls who are glad to get back to school.*

J. Roberts
January 1907

Hon. F. Chatterton:

Just a line to answer you that everything is quiet here now. There has been no danger of a general outbreak of the Indians at all. The Shoshones have been and are as friendly as ever and the Arapahoes, as a tribe, are absolutely trustworthy. I have been apprehensive on account of some renegades, but now all's well. I leave Mrs. Roberts and the children, the two young ladies who are in charge of the pupils and the seventeen little Shoshone girls here in this adobe building, with practically no protection, overnight, without hesitation. I was in Riverton on Sunday, had a hearty service there and organized a Sunday School. It is my opinion, however, that the garrison at Fort Washakie should be maintained until the Indian allotments are made productive...The $50.00 per capita, expected by the Indians, is about to be paid to them and I trust too that the War Department will be induced to retain the garrison at Fort Washakie — at least until the Indian allotments are made productive and (there is) prosperity and contentment...

J. Roberts
January 29, 1907

My dear Bishop (Funsten)
...all is quiet on the Reservation, but old Indians, who are anxious themselves, advise caution until the ground is covered with snow again. It is now dry and frozen. One of my old pupils - the government interpreter - attempted suicide the other day, but fortunately only damaged his hat. He became despondent, owing to the threats against

him. He has plenty of courage which I think I was able to arouse in him for the sake of his three little children and he is now like the rest of us - on the alert for the troublesome ones. The Indians all carry arms and avoid going out at night, some of them even standing guard all night over their homes - but the panic is passing away and next Friday, Washington's birthday, they are to have a feast. I have promised them a beef and we are baking 150 currant loaves of bread for the occasion. This feast I promised them for Easter Monday, but they were anxious to have it sooner. Under the circumstance it was best, perhaps, to consent...

J. Roberts
February 19, 1907

St. Margaret's Hall, Boise, Idaho
February 2, 1907
My dear Mamma,
      We got your letter and all the parcels. I like my dress and other things very much especially the waist material. I have just come upstairs from a Cicero examination. It was very hard.
      Marion and I were very much surprised that there has been trouble with the Indians. We didn't know a thing about it until you told us. All the girls and Miss Hester did but she told them not to tell us and wouldn't give us any other letters except those from one of you. Even now they won't tell us much, though you said everything was all right. How long did you have to stay at the Post? I think it was nice of Mr. Houston to go to meet Papa at Milford...
      Is the post going to be abandoned? We hear that it is and then that it isn't. The girls told us that Miss Hester saved the newspapers that were about the Indian trouble and showed them to the Bishop and asked him to write about keeping soldiers at the Post. I don't know if that is true, the girls sometimes get things mixed up...

With best love to Papa, Gladys and Gwen and yourself,
Nellie (Elinor)

---

in council assembly and quietly and firmly said they were convinced that it was to the best interest of their people that the treaty be made and that they had made up their minds to sign it. This they all did as soon as the opportunity was given them. The fifty dollars per capita expected by the Indians came, and those who had refused their allotments on the ceded portion were assured they would get their allotments on the diminished Reservation. Although all was then quiet, the old Indians advised caution until the ground was covered with snow again. It was the general opinion of those living and working on the Reservation that the garrison at Fort Washakie should be maintained at least until the Indian allotments had been made productive and the plans of the Indian Department had been accomplished with competency and contentment for each individual.

Letters were written to the officials of the War Department to that effect and the fort was not abandoned until 1909.

1910 Virginia Grant and baby— depicting Sacajawea (A.P. Porter)
Star & Crest moon — Ghost Dancers

Chapter 3

Early Living Conditions and Traditions

Since two tribes lived on the Reservation, the missionary clergyman had much to do. The Shoshones were mountain Indians and the Arapahoes were plains Indians; they were not on friendly terms. Their languages, customs and ideas of religion were entirely different, totally unalike.

The Shoshones called Mr. Roberts "Tibo," meaning a stranger. The Arapahoes spoke of him as "Ne-ah-thou," an alien. These terms were generally applied to all who did not belong to their tribes.

To say that Mr. Roberts was received at once into the confidence of the Indians is far from true. But by daily ministrations to the old and infirm, by patient contact with the Indians in their camps, and by kind deeds in the interest and care of the children, he gradually gained their confidence. Then he was spoken of as "Dam-ba-vie," or "Elder Brother." In time he won the unbounded trust and respect of every Indian on the Reservation. For many years, when they were holding council with government officials or making a treaty, the Indians would not negotiate unless he was present.

A letter written by the Rev. John Roberts in 1889 to an Eastern benefactor, six years after his arrival at the Shoshone and Bannock Indian Agency, tells something of the Indian's condition on the Reservation at that time:

Dear Madam,

Your kind letter, with donation, was received a few days ago. On behalf of my poor people, I beg to tender you my heart felt thanks. The money will be devoted to the relief of the destitute, quite a few of whom I see every day. The Arapahoes, for the most part, are very poor and yet not more so than the Shoshones.

I have ascertained the actual amount of rations issued to the Indians. Each one is given one half of a pound of flour and three pounds and one ounce of beef per week. During the winter months the amount of beef was less. They receive a small quantity of baking powder occasionally. Formerly sugar and coffee were given them but none has been given them for two years. For the young and strong this ration was liberal for they could supplement it by hunting a little. Aged and infirm suffer severely. There are numbers of sick and needy, in great distress, in the teepees around.

I have been visiting among them today. Their condition is very pitiful. The cases I could relieve were not many and those only partly. These Indians are passing through, just now, the most trying time they have ever experienced for the reason that the wild game which hitherto has been their support, is now very scarce. They have not yet learned to farm and raise crops. However, they are, this spring, fencing in small farms and the Shoshones have raised a small amount of wheat for the last four years. So far they have no means of having it ground. They pound it with a stone, roast it or boil it but in such a way it is not palatable. They need a mill...I heard Chief Washakie tell an inspector, "I have waited a long time to hear the rumble of a mill. It is one thing to hear before I die."[9] When Washakie consented to settle on a Reservation, he was promised a mill, schools and protection from his enemies. In the early days great injustice was done the loyal Shoshones by allowing the hostile, troublesome tribes much more than was allowed those who had been loyal to the government. Washakie has, on several occasions, led out his warriors to fight for the Whites without pay. He had defended the settlers many times against marauding tribes and several times he has helped the military when it was pressed by overwhelming numbers. Yet he was given half the amount of rations (none by treaty) given other tribes. Washakie once remarked that the Great Father, in Washington, thought more about his enemies than he did about his friends.

I trust that in a year or two their condition will be much improved and that they never again suffer, as they do now, for the bare necessities of life.

It is my earnest desire to remain permanently with these Indians and to do what little I can for them, spiritually and

---

[9] *In 1898 the Shoshones raised one million pounds of wheat. They eventually got the mill which was in use many years. In some seasons it ran day and night.*

temporally. I was sent by Bishop Spalding to organize the Mission and I am thankful to say the work has prospered in spite of many discouragements.

Ever gratefully yours,
John Roberts, missionary

~~~

The first church services held among the Shoshones were in the camps of the chiefs and head men. Under their influence, and knowing that the chiefs listened to the words of the "white robe," others would come together for the service and religious instruction. At his camp, Washakie would have his family and friends called together for that purpose.

Even after services were held regularly in the new little churches, the clergyman customarily went out to his congregation—they were slow to come to him. And yet a group of Indian men would sometimes gather informally and without saying a word, listen to Bible stories and the religious teaching of the missionary for three or four hours. For a long time the teacher was not at all sure of the identity of his listeners since each wore a blanket which covered him, all except the eyes, from head to feet.

With help from the government office, the Shoshones built a council house or dance hall for themselves. This building was one large room. It was made of logs with clapboarding to keep out the weather. The roof was wooden shingles; the floor was the ground with a covering of straw. Straw was also spread on the roof in cold weather. Two guards were stationed outside to call the alarm if and when the straw caught fire from sparks flying up from two wood burning stoves inside the building. The one door was small and opened toward the interior. At the suggestion of the missionary, double doors opening out were substituted for the original one. In winter all meetings and gatherings were held in this building; in summer there was not a place more convenient or pleasant than the banks of a stream in the shade of the trees and willows.

The Shoshones were camped near the council house where they were assembled to celebrate Christmas. Rev. John Roberts held the service and afterward showed, with the kerosene magic lantern, pictures illustrating the Christmas story. Afterward the time was given to social gatherings among themselves and to tribal dancing. A feast was provided by the

Shoshone Council/Dance Hall

Shoshone Mission of the Episcopal Church. There is nothing at all in the tradition of the Shoshone Indians that compares to or that is similar to the Christian celebration of Christmas. They called the festival the "big eating," a name probably suggested to them by their association with the White people.

Many years passed before the members of either tribe accepted or asked for Christian burial for their dead. In 1885 when Baptiste, the son of Sacajawea, died, his body was taken by a few Indians into the mountains and buried. Bazil, the nephew and adopted son of Sacajawea, died in 1886. His body was wrapped in a sheet and blanket, taken by his Indian friends up Mill Creek and placed in a gulch which later caved in and covered the body. Sharp Nose, the last war chief of the Northern Arapahoes who died in 1901, was also buried "in the rocks" by his people. So it was a great step forward when bereaved families, members of which had come under the influence of the church and of Christian schools, began to ask the clergyman to read the burial service for their dead. Many of the old customs would then follow the church service. (Photo page 94)

On one occasion Rev. Roberts was called to hold the burial service for a little Indian girl, a former Shoshone Mission pupil. It was a trying situation for everyone present because within a few yards of the grave there were decomposing bodies of a horse and a dog which had been killed at the graveside of their owner a short time before.

A week later the burial service was read for a young Indian man. After the service, his horse, a beautiful animal, was led to the graveside. It was decorated with bright streamers and painted with gaudy colors. It was frightened and seemed to suspect cruel treatment, for the poor thing gave a shrill scream when a number of Indian men pulled it with ropes to the ground where they strangled it. All this was done so that the owner might have his horse in the "land beyond the setting sun." At another time, two fine horses were killed the same way, one of them saddled and equipped for the long journey to "that other world where the souls of Indians go to be made over."

There is a cave in the north wall of the canyon of the South Fork of the Little Wind River, near the base of the cliff. It was used in the past by the Shoshones as one of their burial places. When a warrior was placed in the cave, his favorite horse, blindfolded, was led to the top of the cliff and forced over the precipice in order to accompany his master to the land of the departed.

The following account was written in 1904 of the funeral of Pedoo whose camp was close to the Shoshone Mission. It shows the change which was very slowly but surely taking place in the attitude of the Indian people:

Mr. Roberts was called to hold the funeral of Pedoo at his home camp. When he reached the camp, there were a number of Indians already there, all wailing, after their fashion. Such lamenting, they thought, was due the dead and so all friends and acquaintances, as they came riding over the prairie, began this mournful crying. But, upon the arrival of the clergyman and until the service was over, all were silent.

The full burial service was read near the dead man's teepee, the front of which was partly thrown open. Then the lamenting began again and went on for some time.

The burial place was far off in the mountains, half a day's journey from the family camp. The dead man's body, wrapped in blankets and bound on a horse, was followed by an escort of friends. When they reached the destination, the body was placed in a cave or crevice of rocks. One of the head men present delivered a charge to the dead, enjoining him not to return to trouble the living or to entice any of his relatives away from earth but to go his way to the abode of our Father, beyond the setting sun, there to be made over and to be made happy in the land of his ancestors.

Pedoo had married a former Mission school girl. She was now in great grief — and well she should have been. Now everything had been given away from her and her two little boys. Her husband had been fairly well off. He had some cattle, a few ponies and a good crop of hay and grain but all had been taken from her, as that was the custom. Each friend took a horse or cow. Her teepee and bedding must be burned or destroyed. Old women carried away, on their backs, heavy loads of flour and other provisions. There had been nothing in the teepee when the missionary arrived except the poor body decked in gorgeous finery, skins and beadwork brought by friends. It was lying on a pallet of bright blankets which would be buried with it. The face had been elaborately painted before death in anticipation of that event. Some of the old Indians have said that in times past, suttee had been practiced.

~~~

Invariably, today the Indians ask for the Christian burial service in the church and at the graveside. Just when the Shoshone burial ground was set apart for that purpose is not known. There were a few graves in the small plot when in 1873, Mrs. Richards and her niece, Mrs. Hall, two women living in the Lander Valley, were murdered by hostile Indians and buried there.[10]

---

[10] *The following is a letter from James I. Patten of Basin, Wyoming, on October 12, 1914 to the Rev. John Roberts of the Episcopal Missions:*

Dear Friend:

I am in receipt of yours [letter] of September 28 asking for information concerning the death and burial of Mrs. L. L. Richards and Mrs. Hall, murdered by Indians at Lander on about September 22 or 23, 1873, according to the best of my recollection.

The hostile Indians had made frequent incursion into our valley that summer. Everyone was busy at the Agency and…inhabitants of the Lander Valley were engaged in tending their crops and getting out poles in the mountains. Some were along the stream fishing and others occupied in various ways. There were observed signal fires in many directions yet notwithstanding, people were markedly indifferent to danger and ill prepared for defense. I believe the only person in the immediate vicinity at the time of the massacre was Lum Williams who was working in the field a half mile up the river; others were Ted Ivans and Chas. E. Fogg and Dr. Miner, about a mile away on the North Fork.

Williams heard the firing which attracted his attention and he looked up his gun and found that he had but a single cartridge in it and none at his cabin. He could, therefore, render no assistance to the unfortunate, besieged women.

Ivans and Fogg saw the Indians approaching but they thought it was someone driving a herd of stock and they got on the roof of their cabin and saw what they concluded was someone driving about 15 or 29 head of horses. They watched for awhile when suddenly an Indian on each horse straightened himself up and Chas. Fogg yelled, "Indians."

There were from 15 to 20 of them and they began circling around and around Mrs. Richards' house, firing through the doors and windows. The women had no firearms. The circling Indians ever drew closer and closer around the cabin and the affair was soon over.

Johnnie Bonsier (?) worked in his field unmolested, knowing nothing of what happened until a searching party went to ascertain if anything had happened to him. All were surprised to find him safe.

About ten o'clock that day of the attack, Dr. Miner came into the Agency having made the journey on foot from the scene of death and notified us of the happening. Word was sent to the absent Lander residents in the mountains and the next morning a party was made up at the Agency consisting of Dr. Irwin, agent, Charles Oldham, Charles Brisett (?), Finn Burnett, Ed Blanchard and myself and wife. We repaired to Lander for the purpose of rendering such aid as we might.

Arriving there we found some ten or twelve people who led us to the cabin of the women. On entering the doorway (there were no doors and windows were only openings in the logs with no sash)…(we found) on the right, in the farthest corner lay Mrs. Hall and in the opposite corner, Mrs. Richards, both lying just as they had fallen from the effects of deadly bullets and arrows of the savages.

After some deliberations, all except Mrs. Patten and myself retired. We were left to inspect the bodies and prepare them for the grave. We learned that after the Indians left and the people came to the cabin, Mrs. Hall was still breathing but unconscious. She lived but a few minutes. Mrs. Hall seemed crouching as from deadly fear, when the fatal instrument of death came. Mrs. Richards must have been standing in a position of defense for her body lay at full length on the dirt floor. As my wife and I turned and lifted her up there was firmly grasped in her right hand a sharp pointed carving or butcher knife.

After all was ready, the corpses were taken to the Agency and on the following day they were both buried in the same grave. Few were there at the service but all showed their sorrow and grief for the victims especially for Mrs. Richards whom all knew so well, whose helpfulness in times when her neighbors were ill or in need of assistance endeared her to everybody who knew her. She was regarded as a woman of high character and her untimely death was sincerely and deeply regretted.

After the tragedy, I wrote articles and the same were published in the New York and San Francisco papers. This soon brought a letter from her husband, L. L. Richards of San Francisco, California. He wrote me that he had left Albion, New York, in 1850, sailed round the horn and if things proved favorable, Mrs. Richards was to have followed him in a year, but that friends came between them and that the result was that she was induced not to join him in California. As the years went by, Mrs. Richards made up her mind to go to California and meet her husband once again.

She was on the overland route when she arrived in the then unsettled Lander Valley. Camp Brown was at that time located where Lander now stands and the commander being in need of someone to take charge of the officers' meals, he made the offer to Mrs. Richards to take the position. Winter was coming on and her plan was to stay there during this season and renew her journey in the spring.

However, she was induced to remain until Camp Brown was removed to Fort Washakie. She had so fallen in love with the climate and country, she thought she would remain, take up a homestead and make her home here. She was erecting a building and had provided herself with chickens, pigs and was doing well financially when the raid occurred. The bedding and many articles of personal value, among other things, two gold watches.

This raid, it seems, was led by a brother of Red Cloud, chief of the Sioux Indians, or at least he was one of the number. After a while these watches found their way to the Sutler's store at the Red Cloud [camp] and when I afterward became Agent of the Shoshones, I had the pleasure of representing the matter of the watches to the Commissioner of Indian Affairs by which steps were taken to secure possession of them and resulted, eventually, in the watches being restored to Mr. Richards.

Any of the old time folks in Lander can show Mr. Nickerson where Mrs. Richards' cabin stood at the time of the raid. The double graves you mention must be hers and Mrs. Hall's grave for there was only (one) such grave there in the Indian cemetery.

I'm writing the above facts entirely from memory, but feel sure they are, including the date, accurate.

Jas. I. Patten

A letter dated 1902, written by Rev. John Roberts to Captain H. G. Nickerson who was then the Indian Agent at Shoshone Agency, asks that "an application be made to the Commissioner of Indian Affairs for an appropriation, for the purpose of fencing in a portion for the Shoshone burial ground." A quarter section of land was surveyed and set apart as the cemetery for the Shoshone tribe by the allotting agent. In this section was included the old burial ground or Agency cemetery where there were about 100 graves. At the head of many of the graves was placed a crude wooden cross. Others were marked with some relic such as an Indian baby's cradle or part of a bedstead, a tent pole, or war bonnet or a warrior's plume.

The Memorial Day[11] service was very important to the Shoshones and was held for many, many years. A gathering of 600 persons was not unusual with many coming from long distances. Some days before Memorial Day, a number of Indians would be seen raking and cleaning

---

[11] *We always joined the Indians on Memorial Day. The cemetery was a beautiful sight when we arrived. The Indians had worked for weeks making wonderful paper flowers. They were dipped in paraffin so that they would last through many showers. The artificial flowers of today can't compare to those that the Indians made, and some still do. They remembered all of the graves. You seldom see a neglected or uncared for grave in an Indian cemetery on Memorial Day. (See also photo page 42)*

the cemetery.[12] The graves were decorated with wild flowers, garden and artificial flowers until the whole scene was a mass of brilliant colors. Then everyone gathered together for the open air service.

The American Legion arrived from Lander on Memorial Day to mark the graves of the Indian veterans and also the old Army scouts. Grandpapa then spoke to the crowd in Shoshone. Each Decoration Day he repeated the promise of everlasting life to each Indian who was now sleeping on the hillside, facing the rising sun. After the service the Indians would come from all over the cemetery to shake hands and to receive a small paper sack in memory of the day, and in memory of the great Shoshone Chief, Washakie. (see page 73, Washakie Lunch)

The following are early veteran soldiers and scouts enlisted in the U. S. Army whose graves are in the Shoshone Indian Cemetery:

Six Feathers - 1887	White Horse
Sargeant - 1889	Matthew No Seep - 1926
John Myers - 1891	Padze Guin - 1927
Arre - 1905	Bob Washington - 1972
So-e-gar - 1907	Eli Wah-wich - 1928
Thad Tid-zump - 1909	Hugo No-yo-ho-go - 1910
Herman Ti-gee - 1911	Little Bob - 1928
George Washakie - 1913	William Allen - 1928
Pe-vo-wa Ute - 1913	Queer Arror - 1929
Panze Wadde - 1915	Newton No-rah - 1929
Appe Barney - 1915	George Enos - 1911
Horace Habbie - 1917	Wit-to-Gant - 1911
Orlo Tin-zo-ne - 1917	Ed Bazil - 1899
John Washakie - 1918	Pusse-ar-ooah
William Surrell - 1918	Zo-op
Addison Bazil - 1904	Bruce English (Dig-goo-ge) - 1931
Earl Nokie - 1906	Allen Zomba
Wah-wan-am-bidde	Hugo Limber (Dag-ga-shua) - 1932
Pegona Martin - 1922	Idja Wam
Claude Ka-ge-va - 1924	Charlie Sargeant
Tab-oon-gwash	Zagwar Allen

---

[12] *The local organization of the American Legion assisted with the usual ceremonies as many Shoshone soldiers and scouts, veterans of the United States Armed Forces, are buried there.*

Pea-doo-rah Tiso-gwe-na   Beaver Hill - 1915
Andrew Bazil   Sego Perry - 1916
Doo-e-vit-see   Jim Wagon - 1917
Perry Barney - 1934   Morah Pogue - 1918
Avan McGee - 1924   Abel Sonnigant
Tosa   Theo Cody - 1923
Quintin Quay   Pedro Passedoah - 1922
George Weasaw - 1904   Peter Pingere - 1928
Orre Momo - 1911   Podze Quin - 1926
To-sat-see - 1907   John St. Clair - 1909
Behugosha - 1903

There are many more to be added to this list, but J. Roberts stopped keeping their names after 1929.

Chief Washakie

Chapter 4

Shoshone Ministry; Shoshone Friends
by Elinor Roberts Markely

In time, a few of the leading men among the Shoshones began to follow the example of their chief by offering their camps as places where services could be held. At one camp, about six miles from the Mission, Moo-ya-vo, a sub-chief under Washakie, would gather his relatives and neighbors to his home to hear his interpretation of the clergyman's Bible stories.

Moo-ya-vo became an outstanding example to his people as an industrious citizen. He had a few cattle and sheep, raised hay and had a fine vegetable garden. He put up a comfortable little cabin around which he planted trees and flowers. Moo-ya-vo was present at a large funeral about the time of the so called Messiah Craze. One of the leaders of the craze was expected to visit the Reservation and the Shoshones looked to the west for a great pilgrim host, the return of the dead. During the earlier period of the Messiah Craze, in the Fall of 1886, there was great excitement on the Wind River. The Indians danced the Ghost Dance frantically all night long for weeks.

Runners had arrived with the startling news that the great host of the dead was advancing from the west and that God was with them. At that time there were great fires in the mountains nearby filling the valley with smoke. For weeks the sunset sky was brilliant orange and red. These phenomena corroborated the strange tidings brought to the Indians and they were wild with a sort of hysteria. Visiting Indians who were here from many other tribes caught the excitement and returned home, mad with the craze that spread among the Sioux, Cheyennes, and even down to the tribes in the Oklahoma Territory. The Reservation was really the Mecca of the Messiah Craze, the cardinal doctrine of which was the return of the dead, the emancipation of the Indians by the return of "great old time" and the annihilation of the aliens.

Moo-ya-vo, seeing the unusually large number assembled at the grave, especially the older Indians, spoke to them, reassuring them and warning them against being deceived by this imposter who claimed he could heal the sick and raise the dead. "That power," Moo-ya-vo told

Moo-ya-vo, Shoshone lay reader and friend of John Roberts

them, "none has but God, our Father, who created us. His only Son, our Saviour, will raise our bodies at the last great day. No Indian medicine man or learned barbarian [White man] can save us. We look to Him, Who created us, and to Him only."

There were other Shoshones, all outstanding in their different ways, who were friends of John Roberts. Herman Tigee, an exceptionally fine man, was one of the best known Indians in Wyoming. He was a close friend, a wise councilor and a trusted lieutenant and chief henchman of Chief Washakie. Tigee was a sergeant of scouts. He was in most of the Indian fights in this state for at least fifty years of his life and always on the side of the White man against hostile Indians. A month before his death, he sent for Rev. John Roberts and asked to be baptized. He said he knew he was going to die and he set the date of his death, almost to the hour.

Gana-wea (Poor or Dull Knife) also known as Quintin Quay, was another Shoshone of sterling character, a highly respected and noted scout. According to official army records, he was "fearless, wise, circumspect and perfectly reliable." His opinion, when expressed to officers in any campaign, was always considered with great attention and full confidence. Gana-wea was present at Fort Bridger with Washakie and Sacajawea when the treaty was signed giving the Shoshones the Wind River country as their Reservation. He believed that he was at least eighteen years of age at the time. Gana-wea was the rider who took the message of the Custer massacre to the telegraph operator, Mr. Robert Hall at Fort Stambaugh, Wyoming. He told his friend, Charles Markley, who was the postmaster at Fort Washakie, that he had ridden from where Billings, Montana, now is to Denver, Colorado, three or four times. When asked if he had been afraid, he said, "If those hostile Indians had found me, they'd have killed me. I rode alone and after dark. In daytime I hid myself and my horse in the brush. Sometimes I stayed at a White man's place but often those places were too far apart."

It was Gana-wea who saved the life of the little Arapahoe boy, the boy who grew up to be the Rev. Sherman Coolidge. Gana-wea enlisted as scout at Camp Brown, Wyoming, for two years. His second enlistment was in the regular army from 1891 to 1894. He died in the late 1940's and was buried with military honors in the Shoshone Indian cemetery near Fort Washakie, Wyoming, with an Episcopal clergyman officiating at the funeral service.

Gana-wea — Quintin Quay (Dull Knife)

John St. Clair was a man well known for his integrity and uprightness of character. He was French and Shoshone. At one time he served as deputy under the Marshal of Wyoming Territory. He raised cattle and was always a good provider for his family, a true example of an industrious and upright citizen. His sons and grandsons grew up to be fine men. They were educated, both academically and vocationally, many of them able to fill responsible positions. One of the grandsons, Wallace St. Clair, retired after thirty years of service in the government office at Fort Washakie. He was also past commander of the Knights Templar of Fremont County, Wyoming. Another grandson, Herman St. Clair, was a member of the Shoshone Business Council. He was an able leader in many civic affairs in the county seat at Lander and in neighboring towns.

John Enos, the patriarch Indian on the Reservation, was a sub-chief under Washakie. He was born in the Flathead country in Montana. His mother was the sister of the late Chief Washakie. His wife was Piegan and French. They had a family of twelve children. She died at Fort Washakie many years before her husband. In his early days, Enos was a great traveler and was noted as a trapper and guide to many important expeditions. He is believed to have been with Bonneville in 1832. He claimed he had been baptized when a little boy by the noted Roman Catholic missionary priest, Father DeSmet. Enos believed he was one hundred and five years old. He died in October, 1915, while accompanying a party of his people on a hunting trip above Brook's Lake in the Wind River Mountains. He was buried in the Fort Washakie cemetery with Father McNamara of St. Stephen's Mission officiating. John Enos was one of nature's own gentlemen, honest, upright, kind, and friendly. He died respected by all who knew him and was mourned by many relatives and descendants.

To-go-te was a Sheep-Eater or Mountain Indian. He, with one or two others of his clan who were more familiar with the mountain passes than the other Shoshones, was designated by Chief Washakie to guide President Arthur and his party from Fort Washakie to Yellowstone Park in August 1883. Since that time, the trail they took over the divide has been known as To-go-te Pass. (Togwotee Pass)

Two Shoshones, Enga-Barrie and Charles Lajoe, assisted the Rev. John Roberts in the work of translating a part of the Book of Common Prayer and a Catechism from the English into the Shoshone language. Charles had been one of Mr. Roberts' pupils from 1883 to 1890.

John Enos, Shoshone Patriarch and friend of John Roberts

The work of making these translations was a most difficult task for the reason that the language is not written and many English words have no counter part in the Shoshone Language. There was no word for heaven; the word "hallowed" and "spirit" were almost impossible to express, and there was just nothing to be done about "forgive" or "sin."

When the translations were completed, printed and first used in the church services, Moon-hav-ve, a Shoshone living near the Mission, was helpful in practicing the reading of them with Mr. Roberts.

Ute was an influential man in the tribe and a typical Shoshone. He was a good friend of Rev. Roberts. He was not as bad as some thought him to be and not quite as good as he claimed to be. Ute, at one time, had a failing for stealing horses. He would even steal from a friend for whom he willingly would do a favor at any time, though not in the least regretting a theft. When Ute was a young man, he, and forty other Shoshones went to the Sioux country on a horse stealing expedition. They were found out and driven into a cave. Only two of them returned to their friends. Ute was one of them. He was severely wounded but managed to hide in the brush until he was able to crawl to a trapper's cabin where he remained while he was recovering. During his stay with the White trapper, he learned a little English; this English was most difficult to understand. Some years later Mr. Roberts met Ute with another Indian in a very lonely place. He expected trouble, but Ute called out the clergyman's Shoshone name, Tab-en-guash, and rode furiously on. It was learned afterward that Ute and his friend were being chased by a detachment of soldiers for some mischief of which they were guilty.

Barbara Baptiste Meyers, Bah-vo-gat-see or Sore Eyes, a Shoshone woman, was a direct descendant of Sacajawea, the Shoshone guide with the Lewis and Clark Expedition, 1804-06. Barbara was the daughter of Baptiste, Sacajawea's son, who was the baby boy that his mother carried on her back across the continent. Barbara married John Meyers, a Civil War veteran who enlisted with the California Volunteers. He was desperately wounded in a battle with the Cheyennes in 1878 on Powder River. At his death, Barbara received a widow's pension from the United States War Department which she drew for forty years. She died December 5, 1931, at the age of 83 years. Her funeral took place at Fort Washakie amid the customary wailing of the Indians. She was buried in the Shoshone Indian cemetery, Rev. John Roberts officiating.

Not many Indian women would go out to work in the homes of White people, but there were a few who did. Betty Narkok was one of the few. She worked as a nursemaid in the lovely old home of Mr. and Mrs. James K. Moore, who was the post trader at Fort Washakie. Betty had much of the care of the four children, and she proved to be very reliable, kind and good. When she left their home to return to her own, she took in and cared for many homeless Shoshone girls and boys.

Maggie Hav-ve, another Shoshone woman, was the laundress at the Shoshone Mission School for many years. Even in severe weather, she walked about a mile from her tepee to the school. After she made the fire in the laundry stove, she took two buckets at a time to the creek for water. At the end of the day she would come to the door, smiling, to ask for her pay. With it tied in a corner of her shawl, she walked two miles to the trader's store to buy something for her family's supper and a little more, which she hoped would last a bit into the coming week.

Chapter 5

Early Services on the Reservation

Church Records in Denver, Colorado, show that the first Episcopal Church service in Lander Valley was held by the Rt. Rev. George Maxwell Randall, D. D., then Bishop of Colorado, Wyoming, New Mexico and "adjoining territories." Randall's first visitation, of which very little is known, was in 1872 and his last in August 1873. The following details of his 1873 trip described in Roberts' 1883 journal were related to Roberts by F. G. Burnett,[13] a member of the armed guard which escorted the Bishop from Fort Stambaugh to the Shoshone and Bannock Agency:

An excerpt from John Roberts' journal dated 1883 reads:

Bishop George Maxwell Randall, Bishop of Colorado, Wyoming, New Mexico and adjacent territories, in August 1873 wrote to Dr. James Irwin, who was then the Agent stationed at the Shoshone and Bannock Agency on the Indian Reservation, that he had an opportunity to pay a visit to the mining camps at Atlantic and South Pass City. He stated he would go there from Denver with a military detachment, and that if Dr. Irwin could furnish him with an escort and transportation, he would go to the Shoshone Agency and meet his people there.

Dr. Irwin responded at once. He manned his ambulance with Charles Oldham, F. G. Burnett and James I. Patten to go to Ft. Stambaugh and get the Bishop. At Ft. Stambaugh, Major Gordon, in command, took charge of the Bishop and his guard of honor and entertained them for the night. On the following morning, with the Bishop, the party started back to Shoshone Agency. As they came down to the head of Twin Creek, these seasoned scouts observed an unusual number of signal fires. Being anxious to avoid contact with hostile Indians, they determined not to take the usual route down through Red Canyon, so they turned to the east and went down Cottonwood

---

[13] *Mr. Finn G. Burnett was the Agency farmer. He told John Roberts of the unflinching way the Bishop endured the hardships of the long, trying journey in the wagon, and he reported that hostile Indians hovered about the party the whole way.*

Creek, striking Little Popo Agie at the Tar Springs now known as the Dallas Oil Field. They arrived at the Agency for dinner at six o'clock. The Bishop's presence softened many hearts and faces. After dinner all retired to the little log building for divine service. There were soldiers, scouts, Indians and hunters all eager to hear the Bishop's message.

The Bishop baptized eleven Shoshone boys and girls. Among them were "Toon-yah-visa-sa," James and "Mah-ve-sip," Richard and "Yahpqui-naa," Nano...?, the children of Baptiste (the son of Sacajawea, the guide with the Lewis and Clark Expedition).

While the service was being held, the Bishop and his congregation were stealthily surrounded by a band of raiding hostile Sioux. The escape of the worshipers from massacre was providential. When the Sioux saw the chapel was full of Whites and Shoshone, they came to the conclusion that these people had taken refuge in the building and were armed and prepared to defend themselves. The Sioux retired as quietly as they had come. Of course, the Bishop and his congregation were entirely unarmed.

When the Shoshones stepped out of the building, they became very much excited for in the brush they saw the imprint of Sioux moccasins, and their horses were all gone. The next spring, Dr. James Irwin was sent by the Indian Office to Pine Ridge, South Dakota, to establish an agency for Red Cloud and his Sioux. When they were assembled in council, the chiefs asked the doctor where he come from. When he told them he came from Shoshone Agency near the high mountains, they said "Why, we were out there last year." "Yes, I know you were," said the doctor. They answered, "In some way you knew of our coming and were all gathered together in that log building, armed and ready to fight us." "No," said the doctor, "not one of us had a gun." That reply from the doctor brought a roar of laughter from the Indians.

I certify that the names of those above baptized, is a true copy of entry made by me in the Shoshone Indian Mission Register of Baptisms. These entries were made from records

Mission House, the original chapel and schoolroom where Right Reverend George Randall conducted services at the Shoshone Agency, 1873. The Building was later moved to Shoshone (Sacajawea's) cemetery, site of this photo.

furnished in 1883 by the Rt. Rev. J. F. Spalding, successor of
Bishop Randall, in office.

John Roberts, B. A.

The small building in which this incident occurred and that now
stands in the Shoshone Cemetery used to be on the bank of Trout Creek at
Wind River just north of the Church of the Redeemer and near the first
government boarding school—the old adobe building established in 1884.
It was originally used as a chapel and as a school room in the 1870's and
1880's. In 1916 it was condemned to be demolished. Mrs. Belnap Nash,
a woman who appreciated the historical value of the building, had it moved
from its original site to the cemetery where it was used briefly as a mortuary
after White burial practices were introduced. The bronze tablet was placed
on the outside wall in memory of the Rt. Rev. George Maxwell Randall,
who held a service there on August 19, 1873.

It is worthy of note that at this time the Episcopal Church had been
the only church at work among the Shoshone or Snake Indians. Under
Grant's administration, the Indians of the United States were allotted to
the different churches. The spiritual and temporal care of the Indians of
this Reservation was also entrusted to the Episcopal Church. With the
addition of these two tribes, the Shoshone and Arapahoe, to Rev. Randall's
already vast diocese, the Bishop assumed a responsibility which eventually
was to cost him his life. The services which Randall held on his trip in
1873 were his last. The rough trip in the open conveyance and other
hardships of the long journey were too much for his over-wrought
constitution. He died at his home in Denver in September.[14]

---

[14] *A second excerpt from John Roberts' journal further describes the frontier condition
the Bishop had to contend with:*

*...the Reservation was then a frontier region (1872-73) subject to constant raids
by hostile Indian tribes. Bishop Randall reached the Reservation traveling in an open
wagon under the escort of an armed guard of four men. They had pressed upon the good
Bishop himself a gun, then he remonstrated by saying he had never shot a gun in his life.*

*When, in addition to the care of this vast diocese, the oversight of two Indian tribes
was entrusted to him, he assumed the responsibility which cost him his life. Faithful unto
death, the aged and hard-pressed pioneer of the Church of God literally died of exhaustion.
Though he reached the agency safely, hostile Indians hovered around his party the whole
of the way. It was the Bishop's last visitation. The hardships and exposure of the journey,
a distance of 150 miles to the railroad, brought on an illness to which his already overtaxed
constitution succumbed. There must have been something very attractive in this Bishop's
character for the early settlers in these mountain valleys always spoke of him with the*

The first Government Industrial School, located at Shoshone Agency close to the Church of the Redeemer. Both Shoshone and Arapahoe students attended this school, which Mr. Roberts was instrumental in building and which he served as superintendent until 1886. Reverend Roberts is the third from the left, back row.

highest personal regard, respect and admiration and yet their knowledge of him was limited to two short visitations, one in 1872 and his last in the next year.

His successors in office, Bishop Spalding, Bishop Talbot and Bishop Funsten followed in his train — equally faithful unto death. The visitation of the Bishop was no vain thing, for with the Bishop goes the Ark of the Covenant.

Bishop Randall, I am told, was a typical Eastern Clergyman and dressed such on his visitations to the remote missions of his vast diocese. He was a gentle saintly man with the courage of a lion. He never faltered in danger, however imminent.

(s) John Roberts

Just less than ten years after Bishop Randall's visitation to the Reservation, the Rev. John Roberts began his missionary work there which was to continue for 66 years.

In 1885, the Church of the Redeemer was built at the Shoshone Agency.[15] Miss Elizabeth Shields, a Baptist, contributed $2,000 for the church to be built in 1884. A letter written by Sherman Coolidge reads: "The front part of the rectory was built in the spring of 1909, and the adobe on back was built the following year." The cross presented to the church is inscribed: "Presented to the Church of the Redeemer, Rev. John Roberts." Under the cross is a card which reads: "This cross is presented to the Church of the Redeemer, Wind River, Wyoming, in loving recognition of services rendered by Rev. John Roberts."

Trees and grass were planted around the new building in 1886 by John Roberts and irrigated by a little stream running through the grounds. The church stood many years on this lovely spot. Informal picnic dinners and many outdoor gatherings often took place in the shade of these beautiful trees. The first government boarding school was just a block east of the church. The church often served the purpose of a classroom.

---

[15] *Through all the years, from 1885 to 1961, services and church school had been held regularly, winter and summer, in this church. Congregations were made up of members of both tribes, White people and very often strangers and visitors. In the spring of 1961, the Church of the Redeemer was moved a mile and a half west, to the grounds of the Shoshone mission. It now faces the Mission which is just across the driveway. The front of the church is flush with the fence which encloses the horse pasture. A good deal of damage was done to the church by the move. The building was insulated with large adobe bricks. These had to be taken out of the walls before it could be placed on the moving rollers.*

The ground upon which the church originally stood was given by the government to the Episcopal Church as long as it was used for religious and educational purposes. This land has been turned back to the United States Government.

Church of the Redeemer, the first Episcopalian Church on the Wind River Indian Reservation, on its original site at Shoshone Agency. It is currently located about 1° miles west, at the Shoshone Episcopal Mission.

All the young Arapahoe catechists received their training through this church where the Rev. John Roberts was rector. These services at the Church of the Redeemer were never for one people more than another or for one tribe more than another. They were attended by the Arapahoes, the Shoshones, the officers and men from Fort Washakie and the people living and working in the vicinity of the Agency.

By the late 1890's the annual Christmas services and festivals held in the Church of the Redeemer were more beautiful and joyous than ever.[16] The children caroling did great credit to their teachers. The pupils from both the Shoshone Mission School and the government boarding school were present which added very much to the success of the gathering. There were two trees laden with gifts which had been provided by generous friends of the mission for the Indians. Each person was remembered. The men received heavy woolen shirts, the women material for dresses, the children toys and clothing. There was candy for everyone.

Attending the service were Shoshones, Arapahoes, and representatives of the Flatheads, Bannocks, Sioux, Crows, Cheyennes, Utes and Paiutes. Such a mixed gathering of Indian tribes would have been impractical not long ago. It was in August 1873 in that little log room, standing 200 feet from where the Church of the Redeemer would be built 12 years later, that Bishop Randall and his congregation were surrounded by a war party of hostile Indians. Mr. and Mrs. F. G. Burnett, who had been members of that first congregation, were now present at this Christmas service and tree.

---

[16] *The following letter from Rev. Roberts' written after the 1893 Christmas service, address the continual need for financial assistance:*

January 18, 1893

My dear Miss Jarvis:

Preparations for Christmas and duties since (are) more numerous than usual, have kept me very busy. Owing to an outbreak of sickness on the reservation, our usual Christmas gathering for the Indian children were not held but our services in the camps were. The Indians were deeply interested in the Advent and Christmas teaching — so that they requested special services in their villages to learn and hear more of the true Messiah. We very much need a Mission room in two of the villages. A log building could be put up in each with the help of the Indians for $200…You have been sending us valuable boxes annually, built us a Church and furnished it, helped to erect a large school building and equipped it for these Indian children…

From the time he came to the Shoshone and Bannock Agency, the Rev. Roberts acted as Post Chaplain at Fort Washakie, holding services in the post hall. The great hall would be filled with stalwart young men in blue. At Christmas time they decorated the hall beautifully with evergreens. Often, a tree for all the children in the vicinity had been planned by the young soldiers. The hearty singing of the familiar Christmas hymns and carols, with their hallowed associations, carried many a one present from that lonely frontier, back to other scenes and days gone by. When the hall burned down in 1900, services were held in the barracks. Church school was kept up, the names of many Indians and White children being on its rolls.

A short account of the Easter service in 1905 reads: "The church was crowded with young Arapahoe and Shoshone boys and girls who had come to join with the Whites in celebrating the anniversary of the Resurrection of our Lord. It is encouraging to see so many of these young people with their intelligent faces, joining heartily in Christian worship and contributing to the offering that other churches and Christian schools might be built."

The first service held in the chapel on the Shoshone Mission grounds, the Chapel of the Holy Saints John, is on record dated December 25th, 1899. Every week day at nine, morning prayer was the custom for all at the Mission. Every Sunday at four Vesper service was held in this chapel by Rev. John Roberts. Many classes of Indian children were confirmed there. Usually the Bishop made his yearly visitation in the spring. Apple and cherry blossoms from the trees growing around the building decorated the chapel. Completing the solemn and beautiful picture were the young candidates in their white dresses and veils standing at the chancel rail, waiting to be presented for Confirmation.

The Mission School's Christmas service for the pupils, their families and friends was always held in the early morning before daybreak. The school children entered the chapel singing, "Hark, the Herald Angels Sing", followed by many other Christmas carols. The Christmas story according to St. Matthew and St. Luke was repeated, from memory by the children. Each child had a bag of candy and a gift. These gifts were nearly always provided by interested members of churches in the Eastern states.

The mothers and grandmothers who were present had nearly all been in school at the Mission and had attended the early Christmas service from the time they were four or five years old and had seen the wondrous sights of their first Christmas tree.

Of the many, many wedding ceremonies performed in this same chapel, only one fell short of the usually happy conclusion! The bride and groom took their places for the ceremony and everything seemed in order until the clergyman said to the bride, "Wilt thou have this man to be thy wedded husband?" Before he could go on with the familiar words, the answer came, unmistakably clear, "No." Possibly the young women didn't understand. "Do you want to marry this man?" "No." The clergyman then suggested that everyone go to the dining room for lunch. But lunch changed nothing. Something was said about the number of horses that had been given to the father of the prospective bride! The young man was last seen walking hurriedly down the lane and the girl drove off with her family.

A real wedding took place after this. The wedding party was quite a large one and since everyone lived quite a distance from the Mission, they came the day before. The ceremony took place after lunch the following day, a very simple ceremony without the usual bride's maid, the groom's best man or the ring bearer. The bride's gown was a bright blue, the bodice, close fitting and long sleeves and low neck. The street length, bouffant skirt had a net over-skirt caught up here and there with pink ribbon and bows. A bandanna, worn around the neck lent a pleasing touch of elegance. The beautifully beaded buckskin gloves, with gauntlets reaching almost to the elbows, matched her buckskin moccasins and fringed leggings. The bride wore her hair in two braids reaching to her shoulders. Her hat was the then very popular tan Stetson, worn with unrolled brim, by all young horse women and cowgirls.

There was a slight interruption in the ceremony when the groom was asked if he had the ring. "Ring? I never bought me no ring! I could-a bought one, I got me a nice bunch cattle up on Big Win' so I could-a sold me a steer and bought her a ring any time, come fall." There is always a way out of a difficulty if it can just be found. It was found.

"Mrs. Roberts, please lend us your ring again."

Chapter 6

Medicine Men and Superstitions

Very rarely at the present time does an Indian patient consult a medicine man. It has taken years of sympathetic, persevering teaching and example to bring about the full confidence that the members of both tribes have in the care they receive in a hospital. Most now seek the doctor's advice and help.

Only those who have worked with the opposition of medicine men know how powerful and far reaching that influence could be. As a religious factor their influence was very strong, not only in the teaching of heathenism as a means of diagnosing and prescribing ways to overcome baneful influences but also in teaching that evil spirits cause illness and death.

A gopher must have come near the camp, because a spell has been cast over a man; a wolf has howled on a neighboring bluff and called the spirit of the sick person away from earth; a horse must be sacrificed in the mountains to break the spell or a wolf skin must be hung up in the teepee to counteract its companion's evil howl. Sometimes the medicine man was puzzled over a case. He had to fall into a trance and explore the land of the dead to ascertain the remedy for the illness of his patient. When he woke up, he had a marvelous tale to tell. If many of his patients recovered, his medicine was strong within him and he would have a good business. Many horses would be given to him. Should he unfortunately lose patients, he would claim that his power was in abeyance, and he would retire from practice for a season until he became charged with it again.

The influence of a bad medicine man could sometimes be pernicious, wicked and cruel, as shown in the story of a case of not many years ago. An Indian family had a little daughter who was extraordinarily precocious. The little girl walked and talked when unusually young; a medicine man visiting the family noticed this. He called his friend aside and broke the terrible news to him that the little one was not his own child but that of an evil spirit who had kidnapped his daughter and had entered her body with the cruel purpose of bringing dire calamity upon her father and his family.

He advised the father that the only way he could save himself from disaster was to take the little child far away to some lonely spot on the mountain where she belonged and abandon her.

The parents were actually on their way with the child when one of their neighbors, To-ya-ri-bo, met them. They told him their pitiful story. To-ya-ri-bo told them that he believed in the Son of God who was stronger than all evil. Though he had a large family of his own, he begged the parents to give the child to him, which they gladly did. To-ya-ri-bo brought her to the chapel of the Holy Saints John at the Shoshone Mission to be baptized. Then he took the little girl home with him.

This true story is one of many similar ones. An Indian who lived close by the Mission came pleading for $2.00 to pay a medicine man to drive away the sickness that had come to his little son. The little boy was sick with some passing ailment, but the medicine man said the little fellow's spirit had gone to play with the spirits of departed playmates on the other side of the mountain. By hideous howlings and incantations carried on in the dead of night he claimed he had succeeded in enticing the boy's spirit back to his body.

A Shoshone woman lost her daughter to tuberculosis. She blamed the death on the spirit of a rejected suitor. She was sure that he had procured a magic powder from a medicine man for the purpose of harming the girl when he sprinkled it in her footprints after she walked by.

It was customary in both tribes during their former nomad life to abandon their old people when they became helpless and a burden. Usually these old people were provided with a teepee, a supply of meat and roots and left to their fate.

Under the tyranny of such ideas, these people lived in constant fear and terror.[17] But the dominant superstition that oppressed them was the great dread of an invisible, malignant demon they called Nin-im-be, who they thought was the cause of most misfortunes and sorrows. This nemesis, after obtaining the name, age and other particulars concerning an Indian, took to following him and shooting at him or some member of his family with invisible, flint-pointed arrows. These arrows caused no outward

---

[17] *John Roberts was visiting with some people who had come to talk about the Indians. They asked him if he ever became discouraged when the Indians clung to their old ways. He answered, "Not at all. I am a Welshman and civilization was brought to Wales more than four hundred years ago and many are still clinging to the old ways and old superstitions. Change takes a long, long time."*

wound but were evil in their effect, causing sickness and death. In the case of a succession of misfortunes or deaths in his family, the ill-fated man struck camp some dark night and escaped to the mountains where he hid for many weeks, sometimes for months. Nin-im-be, having lost him, might pursue someone else. For this reason, one of the chief characteristics of a Shoshone used to be his abnormal secretiveness and illusive nature. The old tyranny of this superstition has quite recently loosened its hold on its victims, and a more open, straight forward attitude toward life has taken its place, brought about by a close contact with civilization.

The little owl that lives in the burrow with the prairie dog also gave the Shoshone some concern. A group of White boys were playing with some little Indian boys. When they tried to catch one of the small owls for a pet, they were severely reprimanded by their Indian playmates to leave the owls alone! The little owl was the brother-in-law of the prairie dog, Tin-zi- En-deach, and anyone catching him or playing with him would surely "go crazy."

Chapter 7

The Sundance

John Roberts wrote of the Sundance as follows: This past June [1892], the Indians have been very busy. Day after day their wagons, bound from the mountains west of the Shoshone Mission, to Fort Washakie, have passed loaded with logs. Fifteen hundred cords of fire wood were called for by the military authorities at the fort. The Shoshones and Arapahoes worked earnestly to supply the wood required and before the end of the month eleven hundred cords were delivered. The timber had to be hauled a distance of eight to ten miles. It was procured in steep and almost inaccessible places in the mountains.

The work then stopped for a short time in order that the Shoshone might hold their annual Sundance. This ceremony is one of the most ancient of their sacred rites. It took about five days, the first of which were devoted to preliminary arrangements. Long, straight poles, brought from the mountains, were used in the construction of a circular pavilion.[18] On horseback, the men of the tribe escorted the

---

[18] *It took about two days for the Sundance pavilion to be prepared and for the Indians with their camps to all assemble. A number of the Indians would go to the mountains and get sturdy poles to construct the main framework. They then made a large circular skeleton framework around a center pole. Twelve large poles were placed from the center pole to the outer frame and secured. The outside frame was covered with brush and small trees, except for the eastern side which was left open to face the early morning sun.*

Each dancer had a small opening, or an open entry in which he stood when not dancing up to the center pole and back. The women had brought sweet smelling young sage and grasses to make a pallet for their dancer in his cubicle. This filled the entire pavilion with the delicious smell of sage, which added to the smell of the large bonfire which was kept going at all times on the eastern side of the center pole where the singers and men that beat the drums were. The Indian women who sat on the ground and sang, would each have a small bundle of young willows in hand, which they shook up and down in time to the music. The Indian men who took turns at the drum would sing and beat the drum so softly you had to hold your breath to hear the sounds; then they would increase the tempo until the sound would almost engulf your whole body. The sounds, the

Dancers approaching the center pole at the Shoshone Sundance.

smells and the dancers' beautiful beaded decorations all added to the exhilaration of the event.

For years my family went to the opening night of the dance. My father and mother knew the names of all of the dancers. They knew if it was the first time for a dancer, or if he had danced many times. Sometimes they would see a guest dancer from another tribe that had joined the Shoshones. The evening of the opening of the dance was one of great anticipation for everyone. There was usually a long wait after sundown as each dancer was preparing to enter the dance. After a wait, we would first hear the whistles, softly blowing and then the big center drum would begin. The dancers came out of the dusk and circled the lodge before entering and taking their places. My parents would go around and talk to some of the Shoshone people, and I was always proud that they could converse so easily in the Indian language. This when I was very young, made me feel more like we were a part of all the events.

---

wagon on which the poles were carried until they came off the mountain and reached the valley. The young men then dressed as though they were going on the old time warpath and rode all over the foothills and valleys engaging in a sham battle made really quite terrifying by the noise of the shouting and rifle fire. At the site of the dance, the center pole was set up first with a buffalo head, a piece of buffalo hide or several eagle feathers fastened at the top of it. From the center pole a ring of smaller poles were placed, reaching from it to posts also placed in a circle and some feet apart forming the outside of the pavilion. These poles were not named for the twelve apostles as is so often erroneously stated.[19] Small booths where the dancers rested were made of green branches, skins and perhaps a blanket, just inside the outer ring of posts.

The significance of the buffalo head on the center pole of the Sundance tabernacle would be similar to that of a sheaf of wheat on the altar of a Christian church at a special harvest or Thanksgiving service. I remember asking prominent Indians when I first came on the Reservation what the buffalo head meant to the Indians. They could give me no definite answer other than that at times a medicine man would claim that a buffalo had appeared in a dream to him, demanding a Sundance. Sage and Drives-down-hill are very reliable men, both on U.S.

---

[19] *My mother was adamant in her opinion that not only did the twelve poles not stand for the Twelve Apostles but also that any concept of the Sundance having been Christianized was untrue.*

Army pensions. A story that they would tell would not be 'made up' to suit the occasion and Otto Hungry was a straight forward, intelligent interpreter.

In another entry entitled, *"Shoshone Sundance: A feast of tabernacles called by them 'Dag-ooy-ar-roi' or 'Standing-thirsty dance,'"* Roberts continued his description. "For three consecutive days and nights, they dance, abstaining from all food and drink, until they faint from exhaustion, when they claim they see visions and revelations in their delirium."

"A fire was built near the center pole as soon as it grew dark. At the right and in the wide opening which was always in the east, the families of the dancers, guests from other Reservations and all other spectators, stood watching. At the left were the men singers and drummers; near them sat a group of women, singing and waving green branches in time with the drum."

Many teepees and tents were pitched near and around the Sundance pavilion. Here the Indians had moved for the duration of the festivities. For relief from the hot sun, many of them built a temporary shade of green willows.

About dusk on the evening the dance began, the dancers (whose bodies had been covered with a thin coating of white paint) came from their camps and forming a line, walked slowly around the pavilion three times before taking their places inside. Each one had a whistle made from the thigh bone of a crane with eagle feathers tied on, upon which was sounded as they walked a single smooth note over and over again. This same whistle tied on a buckskin string around the owners neck was used in the dance but with a very different sound—a plaintive, peculiar chirping note resembling that of a young bird in distress. With their gaze fixed on the buffalo head at the top of the center pole, hopping like birds, the dancers pipe on their whistle and advance and retreat from it to their booths. They dance with short intervals of rest for three days and nights without food or water. Their costume is a shawl fitted as a skirt or apron which hangs from the waist to the ankles. It is elaborately trimmed with designs in beads, bands of buckskin, shells or metal pieces, and the upper part of the body and the feet are bare. Paint of various colors has now taken the place of the white paint worn by the dancers during the opening ceremony.

The scene, especially viewed in the light of the fire at night, is a strange one. The smell of smoke from many camp fires, with the good smell of crushed sagebrush and willows which the wives and mothers carry in for the dancers to lounge on, is over all. The songs of the Sundance are quite different from those of the Round Dance and Wolf Dance. The music, the rhythm of the drum, the whistles and the chorus of the men's and women's voices will entice the visitor back year after year.

Toward the close of the dance, several of the dancers faint from sheer exhaustion and weakness. They claim they see visions and have revelations while in this semi-conscious state, which they afterward make known for the benefit of the tribe. Often a patient comes in or is carried in to be healed by the medicine man. He stands with bared head or lies on his pallet by the center pole. The medicine man strokes the pole, then his patient with his eagle feathers. He lifts up both hands toward the pole, and prays. Sometimes this ceremony and variations of it are repeated several times before the patient turns and walks away. If he is bed-ridden, he is usually carried to one side and left to rest.

The rising sun is greeted by all the dancers coming to face the opening at the East where they stand and sing some strange song in the minor key, then, together they blow their whistles. Occasionally there is some diversity in this ceremony. Upon retiring to their booths, they make ready for the day with fresh paint.

At the breaking up of the dance, gifts of horses, blankets and beaded buckskin articles are made to visiting Indians. A Wolf Dance that evening is a very important affair which everyone attends."

At one time the Department of Indian Affairs prohibited the Sundance on the Reservation, but the dance was in abeyance a few years only. Since then it has been held regularly every year.

The Sundance practiced by the Arapahoes is quite similar to that of the Shoshones. One difference is that the Shoshones dance from their booths to the center pole and back while the Arapahoes stand by their booths, blowing their whistles and keeping time to the music with a slight movement of the knees. Around the center pole, at the Arapahoe Dance, are seen kettles and bowls of food. No food is seen at the Shoshone Dance.[20]

---

[20] *The dancers would come out of the lodge and face the rising sun with the eagle whistles blowing softly and then the sun would finally come up and be greeted by a row of Indians with arms upraised welcoming the new day. Watching this ceremony gives one a glimpse of the history of this land long before European exploration.*

My family belonged to the minority race and to return to where I grew up did not always mean that I would be recognized and greeted.

Reverend Roberts and family were attending the Arapahoe Sundance. The dance was usually held not far from our home and all night long we could hear the singers and the drum. Before daybreak my sister and I would often catch our horses and ride the mile or two to the sunrise ceremony.

Chapter 8

Early Education and the Episcopal Mission Boarding School for Shoshone Girls

"Roberts Mission" 1890 to 1949

When Bishop Spalding sent John Roberts to Wind River in 1883, it was initially to organize an Indian Mission. Shortly thereafter, with the cooperation of the U.S. Indian Agent Dr. J. Irwin, Roberts established the government Wind River Industrial School for Indian children. This boarding school for both Shoshone and Arapahoe boys and girls was built in 1884 during the administration of President Arthur, who assigned the spiritual care of these Indians to the Protestant Episcopal Church. In such an isolated place as the Agency where living conditions were so lacking in any degree of comfort or convenience, it was most difficult to get workers. So preaching, teaching, cooking and nursing were all part of John Roberts' work day. John Roberts continued as superintendent of this school until the fall of 1886; there were between 80 and 90 boarders on the school roll at that time.

While waiting for the first government boarding school to be built, the Indian school boys shared Mr. Roberts' cabin. The only furnishing was a carpet padded with straw underneath. This made a fairly good bed, but the fact that the smaller boys had spent the early evening on the bank of Trout Creek hunting and catching skunks was not conducive to a good night's rest.

The Government Industrial School, Wind River Agency was built on the banks of Trout Creek one-half block east of the Church of the Redeemer. It was a one-story, adobe building with a few windows which had heavy iron bars[21] across them. The government supplied no furniture for the pupils' use — no tables, chairs or bedsteads. The policy of the Indian Department was that the older boys should make all the furniture. So, with one horse, Rev. Roberts and several of the boys went to the mountains and "snaked" down logs to build their furniture. Neither the

---

[21] *Iron bars were placed on the windows to protect the children inside from the possible attack of hostile tribes and also for the purpose of keeping the children safely in school at night.*

Government Industrial School

Missionary nor the Indian boys had any training or experience in the use of carpenter's tools; but the need was desperate, and somehow they made the necessary pieces. All this was accomplished without verbal communication. Perhaps it was fortunate that wood was used in all the stoves in the building, and the "mistakes" could be put to good use.

In 1892 a new government school was built.[22] This school was placed on the land not too far from the hot springs. The original building has been added onto many times, and new buildings have also been constructed here. The school is still in use, although almost all of the old buildings have now been replaced.

The dormitories and classrooms of the new school were bright and airy. There were many acres of land in connection with the school where the older boys learned about farming and stock. However, even under favorable conditions, civilization and school life was hard on the Indian children. Fifty percent of the children died. Statistics on the death rate of Indian children in the early years of school life show the following:

Identity	Children in Government School	Deaths
Ute	5	4
John Weed	1	1
Tabanguash	3	3
White Horse	3	3
Nokok	4	3
Tinzone	3	2
Win	4	1
Washakie	7	1
Rigee	3	1
Peahroah	5	4
Bishop	1	1

---

[22] *The old school building was then used as the Agency office until it burned in 1906. Many valuable papers and records burned with it.*

Staff at first Government Industrial School
First Row:Miss Roberts, assistant teacher;Mr. Egbert, industrial teacher
Second row: Mr. Roberts, principal;Miss Mertin, matron;Miss Hinckly, assistant matron;Mrs. Roberts, assistant teacher;Miss Russel, seamstress
Third row: Rev. Coolidge, Arapahoe Minister;Mr. Goodmonson, assistant teacher;Mr. J. E. Chadderton, cook

The following letters reflect this same concern:

To Mr. Wadsworth, Government Official, January 9, 1901:

I thank you sincerely for your great kindness in taking up the matter of the Shoshone pupils. I have written to the Hon. Commissioner about the difficulty of keeping these children alive in school....

To Major Dickson, U.S. Supervisor of Indian Schools on January 30, 1901:

There is one matter of serious importance that I would respectfully call your attention to, that is to the very heavy death rate of Shoshone pupils in our schools. I attribute the great mortality to nothing other than of effect of our civilization on their wild natures.

In 1901 Rev. Roberts wrote the Indian Department:

The heavy death rate of the pupils is undoubtedly due to the effect of civilization upon them. In school they have good care, wholesome food well cooked. They have plenty of fresh air, outdoor exercise and play. Yet under these conditions, in school, they droop and die, while their brothers and sisters, in camp, live and thrive.

In this letter, Roberts asked for permission to allow the pupils to spend some time at home for intervals during the school year. After much delay, his recommendation was allowed. The improvement in the health of the children was marked and almost immediate.

During the years when Rev. John Roberts was superintendent of the first government boarding school, he saw the great need for a church boarding school. This was made possible when in 1887, Chief Washakie, not yet knowing much about the Episcopal Church, made a personal gift to Rev. Roberts of 160 acres of land for the site of a permanent school for Shoshone girls. In making this generous donation, Washakie surely had the welfare of the children at heart. He had said some years before, "Our hope is in the children and young people. The old people can't hear." He realized the value of educating them in Christian schools where they would be given the opportunity of becoming self-supporting citizens. Washakie

Wind River Boarding School of 1892 ~ Replaced the Government Industrial School. The portion at the extreme left still stands as part of Fort Washakie School.

said to John Roberts that he believed the children must be educated to live in the Indians' changing world. Roberts felt that the girls should be the first to be educated because they would return to the camps, establish homes of their own and teach the new generation. He later tried to raise money to help educate Shoshone boys as well.

Influenced by the spiritual teaching of the Rev. John Roberts, Washakie was baptized. He was very anxious that the members of his tribe accept the Christian faith and be baptized. In one of his messages to his people he said, "One thing I want to see and my heart will be at peace: I want to see the church and school built by the 'white robes' for my people."

Washakie's gift of land was ratified by an Act of Congress and also made official by the Shoshone Tribal Council a few years later. By this ratification, any gifts made to the school subsequently could "never be alienated from the purpose for which they were given."

It is regrettable that no picture was taken of the laying of the cornerstone of the Shoshone Episcopal Mission School in 1889. At that time the only camera was owned by a man living 150 miles away. The picture would be most interesting today. Not only were all the Indians present, dressed in the most colorful costumes of that early time, but the whole garrison from Fort Washakie was in attendance. Many of the old and well-known pioneers were among the congregation. Bishop Ethelbert Talbot and other clergy, all wearing their official robes, were present. Following the service, a feast of roast beef, many loaves of bread, and coffee without measure was served to the guests. There was the smoking of the ceremonial pipe and talks and dancing until late at night.

The site was a lovely one on the west end of the Reservation at the foot of the Wind River Range and on the open prairie. At that time not a fence nor a farm was in sight, and only a few teepees could be seen along the banks of Trout Creek. The place was a sacred one to the Indians. It was where many of their most solemn assemblies and religious dances had been held, on the very ground they were giving for religious and educational purposes. It was known to trappers and early pioneers many years ago. Some had attempted to settle on it and though they were defended by the Shoshones, many were killed and others were driven away by hostile bands of raiding Indians.

~~~

The Shoshone Mission was a two-story structure; the bricks in the main building were made on the grounds. Many windows made the rooms bright and cheery. Ceilings were high and like the walls, all plastered a dazzling white! The one fairly large dining room was used by the Indian children, visiting families and was also the mess dining room.[23] It was the schoolroom for a number of years and, in inclement weather, evening prayers were held in this same room. The Chapel of the Holy Saints John[24] was built on the Mission grounds in 1899 but a good many years passed before a school room,[25] a second dormitory[26] or bathrooms[27] could

---

[23] *The dining room was full of large tables with stools for the girls to sit on. This was the place where they ate, a place to play when it was storming, and a place for them to gather in the morning for daily prayers and schooling in housekeeping and sewing.*

There was a small laundry room to the north. The laundry stove was in the middle with sad irons placed in a slant, in grooves around it. Round wash tubs hung on the walls. Water was brought in from Trout Creek, heated on the kitchen stove and then carried to the tubs. All of the girls had a bath two or three times a week. This was just the beginning of the work. After all the bathing was completed, clothing for twenty-five or more girls had to be washed and hung outside to dry, sometimes in freezing weather. To add to difficulties, the water was very hard; it left a gray scum on the top of the wash tubs. I remember a wonderful invention which sat on the back porch. It was a new washing machine, like a large, round wooden box. A few clothes would be placed in it and hot water added with soap, then everyone in the mission would have a turn pushing the wooden paddle up and down. After much fuss about whose turn it was, spilt water, and attempts to skim off some of the hard water scum, the few clothes were finally proclaimed clean. It was discouraging work when one stopped to look at the huge pile of washing to be done everyday.

[24] *The chapel altar had cloths on it as it does today and the organ still stands where it always had up near the front of the room. My mother played this organ every Sunday for many years before I was born and as long as my grandfather lived. Even the baptismal font given in memory of Chief Washakie is still in place. A path made out of cobblestone, which my grandfather laid by hand, and most of the old orchard trees that once made a canopy from the mission building to the chapel are gone, but the chapel has been saved and cared for with great love all of these many passing years.*

Near the chapel is the small log cabin, which was always called "The cottage." This was where my grandparents and their five children lived while the mission building was being constructed. I remember going into it as a child and looking at the scant pieces of furniture, and the few old pictures on the wall. I believe my grandfather built the small cabin, in part, for a rich young lady that came from the East to live and work among the Indians. (Grace Weatherbee married the man known as the Arapahoe Preacher, Sherman Coolidge.)

Two churches have been relocated around the Mission's circular drive. Facing west is the old Church of the Redeemer; the first church my grandfather built was originally on the banks of Trout Creek east about a mile and a half near the old Agency, next to the

Shoshone Episcopal Mission School, Trout Creek

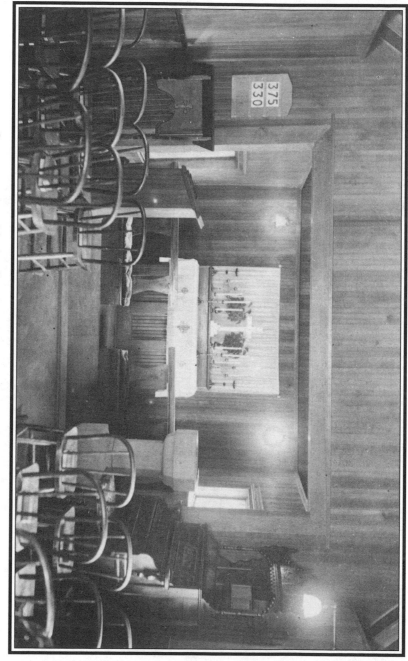

Contemporary photo of the virtually unchanged interior of the Chapel of the Holy Saints John.

first Government school. Services were held there for the two tribes and the troops from the Fort. The land on which it stood was given to the church by the Indians. Two small rooms were added on the side of the building. This was where my grandmother came as a bride and where my grandfather was taken for his burial services after working on the reservation for sixty-six years. Old trees still mark the spot where it originally stood.

Another church, which was built many years later at Fort Washakie, was also moved to the mission grounds. Saint David's was named for the patron Saint of Wales in honor of my grandfather. This had a vicarage built near, but was never used by my grandfather and is not a part of early history on the Reservation.

[25] The schoolroom was added to the mission building in the later years. School had initially been held in the chapel where a moveable partition could be put up and taken down every time a church service was to be held. I remember the schoolroom looked huge to me as a child. It was completely filled with desks; I can't remember a teacher's desk, but then, she never had time to sit down!

All grades went to school here and some of the older girls taught the equivalent of high school. The school bell rang at one o'clock and classes lasted until well after five o'clock in the afternoon. How tired the little four and five year olds must have been before the day in school ended. The Indian girls learned to read, write and do math before I did in the District school near Fort Washakie. These Indian children had much more to learn than the White children. First grade pupils had to translate the reading chart in their heads, trying to deal with words and stories which had nothing to do with their world. After they had figured out what the White children in the pictures were doing, they then had to find what English word to use.

[26] The first and main dormitory was upstairs on the north side of the building. Several years ago when I returned to the mission, I listened and heard the same sound, the lonely sound of the ventilators in the ceiling which I had heard as a child. It sounded like the wind wailing for the people now long gone from the old building. A window had been broken and a curtain was blowing softly back and forth out of it. I remember the rows of beds, the white spreads pulled up smoothly on each cot. The little Indian girls are now grown, some of them gone. The wind in the ventilators and the blowing of the curtain seem to define this as the end of an era.

A smaller dormitory was added on many years later at the west end of the hall, extending out over the kitchen. This room was greatly needed because each small cot was already holding two girls each night, a comforting arrangement for the small five year old girls. They were away from their homes for the first time, their parents and everything that was familiar. An older girl sleeping with them was probably the only thing that made school life bearable. Each dormitory had a coal stove. These needed careful tending all night because of the severe winter cold and the danger of fire with the cots so near by.

[27] After many years of carrying water up from Trout Creek in buckets, an old hand pump was installed in the kitchen. Everyone was delighted with the new well and the red pump. However, this water was also very hard and almost impossible to use. Years later a part of the kitchen was set aside for the bathroom. This was many years too late in coming as my grandmother was dead and the school had been closed. To realize the work that had been accomplished at the mission, one needs to remember the lack of water or conveniences which might have made things a little easier.

The "outside bathrooms," as we were taught to call them, were a far distance away, and the ground between them and the mission was a sea of deep gumbo mud in the *springtime. There were about four of them. All had a small board on the outside with a nail in the middle, and when we came out we would turn them across the doors so that they wouldn't swing and bang in the Wyoming wind. Many times, with much giggling and whispering, a girl would sneak up and close the board while someone was still inside. It would seem like an eternity before anyone would come running back to let you out. This fun was never forbidden because none of us told the adults.*

---

be added to the building. Each year 25 Shoshone girls between the ages of five and eighteen lived here during the week. On Saturday mornings they were taken home by their parents who returned them on Sunday afternoon in time for baths, the vespers service, and supper.

The daily routine began with breakfast at seven followed by a detail of girls to different duties such as dormitory, kitchen, or laundry work. At nine the chapel bell rang for morning prayers and an hour of religious instruction. The pupils memorized a number of chapters from the Bible. They learned the Catechism, the Lord's Prayer, the Creed and the Ten Commandments in English and in their own language. They learned to earn their Lenten offering by doing little chores for which they were paid. Only a few figures are available for the record, but they are well worth noting. The children's Easter offering for 1933 was $87.80; for 1934, $97.50; later the amounts $98.00 and $108.00 were given in two different years. These children held nothing back of their earnings; they gave their all.

There were two classes a week in cooking and sewing. Handwork, embroidery, drawing, and writing came very easily to the Indian children. Academic classes were held after lunch where the regular county courses of study were followed. To combat homesickness, a circular cabin of logs in the fashion of a teepee was built in the Mission yard. A fire could be built in the middle of the dirt floor with the smoke escaping through an opening in the roof. In this imitation teepee the girls were allowed to practice their native songs and dances during that wonderful hour between supper and evening prayers (This really historic little building has recently been torn down and even the lumber disposed of — in the cause of a questionable progress). One evening a week, the older girls were encouraged to exercise their skill in beadwork. Buckskin and beads were furnished them, and many winter evenings were spent happily at work making beautiful beaded bands and purses.

This is Beatrice Crofts' account of the Shoshone Mission and her remembrances of it as she looked back during the week of the celebration

Outbuildings of Shoshone Episcopal Mission School (south of main building) "Teepee" at left was built by Rev. Roberts for children to play and be Indian. A fire could be built inside, and the older girls would sometimes take beadwork to do.

of John Roberts' arrival one hundred years before and as she looked at it in 1983:

  I had not been back to the Mission for many years. Quite by accident, I learned that the Episcopal Church was going to have a memorial celebration in honor of my grandfather's arrival on the Reservation one hundred years ago. This sent me back again to look at the old buildings on the north banks of Trout Creek.

  As we drove into the mission grounds I felt that I had come home to a hallowed spot. I walked onto the old front porch, looked at the large door and noticed the same bell fastened to it; you would turn the knob and it made a soft ring. The door was never locked and I can never remember anyone ringing the doorbell. Visitors just walked in as I now did. I almost expected to see my grandfather still sitting there on a straight backed chair near a small radio. When he was in his nineties he had often sat in here keeping up on the news with his radio, as he was blind and could no longer read. The room was rather dark and almost cold in it's severity. His old desk was near the door and a few old chairs were placed around the room, in preparation for visitors. A few old Indian men would come in and silently sit and exchange a few words and then quietly slip away. This had once been a very busy room; too many visitors, as my grandfather tried to get all of the many reports and letters written in any spare time he had in his busy schedule. He was now blind and lonely, though always very careful not to show how lonely he was in the last years of his life. He would take his walking stick and walk through the fields and test the soil for moistness. These fields had once raised tons of hay which he fed to his vast cattle herd. He raised these cattle to support the Mission.

  I left the office room and continued down the hall. This hall seemed to be very narrow and dark. I remembered it as being very large when I was a child. The room next to the "office room" at one time had a very large table in it. This is where the Roberts family ate, the matron, the teacher and perhaps in busy haying season, two or three hired men. This table served many purposes beside being a place to eat. Before

Decoration Day, as Memorial Day was then called, small brown sacks covered it. In each sack, we would place an orange, a few raisins, soda crackers and a piece of yellow cheese. All of the family and some of the older Indian girls helped to fill these sacks which were called "Washakie's lunch." This is what he always bought at the Indian Trader's store to carry with him. My grandfather started the tradition of passing out these sacks to each Indian, after Memorial service was held at the Indian's cemetery. The grandchildren were allowed to help pass out these sacks as a great honor, or a sign that we were now old enough to have this responsibility.

I walked on to the next room, the kitchen, and went down the old sandstone step at the end of the hall. The old step used to be worn down in the middle from years of little Indian children going up and down as they went about their daily living. My grandfather called it his measuring stone. He showed it to me and explained that it had been flat at one time across the top, and that it would always be a lifetime measure of the many footsteps that had been going about the mission's business. Unfortunately, this stone had now been "repaired" with cement.

The school was in session 55 years. By stocking the farm with cattle and horses,[28] sheep, pigs and chickens, ducks and geese and by growing all the vegetables and fruit used by the pupils, the school was almost entirely self-supporting when it was closed in 1945.[29] As early as 1897, one hundred tons of hay were grown on the Mission farm. Aside from

---

[28] *The cattle sheds and barns, huge vegetable garden, and a small cabin where the hired man slept were set back from the main Mission building. The barns were forbidden ground. They usually held steers being fattened for butchering or a penned up bull. Large wooden tubs filled with bran sat in the corral. What wonderful times we had jumping into the corral, grabbing a handful of bran to cram in our mouths and jumping up on the fence before the animals reached us. Then we would dare the next one to try it. The bran was a delightful treat, more so after the risk taken to grab it. We soon stopped this game when one of us discovered small wiggly worms in the bran — just about the same color as the grain!*

To the west of the Mission building were the buggy sheds. These also afforded a wonderful place to play. We would sit in one of the buggies and the Indian girls would all get hold of the tongue and pull us all over the Mission land; then we would get out and

give them a ride. It added to the excitement and fun if we would pull it quickly enough and spill a few riders into the irrigation ditch. I'm sure this didn't help the buggies but it did keep us all quite busy for a few hours until the bell rang for Vespers on a Sunday afternoon. Then we all sat in the chapel and were very well behaved with the buggies placed back in their respective places.

[29] *There is little left of the old barn, just a shell to show where it once stood. There is nothing to show where the huge vegetable garden was. It was one of the main sources of food for all of us. The buggy shed is gone and the buggies that my grandfather used in his work are no longer on the grounds.*

being a source of revenue to the school, growing hay provided a valuable learning experience for Indians who, whenever possible, were hired to harvest crops of hay and grain. A few years later the Mission was surrounded by Indian farms which were not very extensive but did support the growth of hay and grain — a hopeful sign.

Operating a farm in connection with the school to help support it was a very wise measure. The church had very little money — for a period of ten years there was no money from the church at all. Before the Indians received per capita payments, they were too poor to give any financial help for the education of their children.

In reply to a request made by Bishop Thomas asking for a financial history of the Shoshone Mission, reference was made to the old account books. The government paid for the support of the school from September 1893 - 1899, the sum of $13,657.39, which made a small average per annum. After that contract expired in June 1899, the Board of Missions made a grant of $1,500.00 per year to Bishop Funsten for the school's support. This grant was generously allowed until December 1911 when it was reduced to $900.00.[30]

[30] *The following letter written by John Roberts in 1893 to some of his old classmates in college illustrates the school's predicament:*

When I look back on the last 17 years, I have every cause to be thankful. I have no regrets. You know my heart was always set on the distant out posts of Christ, seeking a new field where no one had been before. I found it here. I wish to appeal to my old friend for a little help for my work here. Will you not assist me?

We have erected a nice boarding school, large enough for the 20 Indian girls, but we have no room for boys. We need a dormitory and schoolroom for boys, but first we want to clear off the debt on our present building which amounts to $700.00. Will you not try to help me clear it off? I shall be very grateful to you, if you will. I have no one on this side of the world to appeal to. No treasury to draw on. All the money we have spent here has been contributed by private subscription. It was a great undertaking to erect such a building as the one we have here. The bricks we had to make right here, some of the lumber had to be brought a distance of 1000 miles and the tin for the roof came from Old Wales. Connected with the Mission, we have a farm of 160 acres. The land was given to the Church by Chief Washakie. It is doing a grand work in the way of civilizing these Indians. The grim old warriors are taking to farming with great determination. There are now little farms all around us. They have given up hunting and have gone to work. Just now they have moved up to the mountains back of the Mission to get 2000 loads of fire wood for the soldiers at Fort Washakie, the military garrison on the Reservation. Times are changing here. They would no more do this than fly when I first came among them. Fifty-two young fellows are now enlisted as soldiers here. I trust that before long some of my boys, who are splendid young fellows, will be able to take up my work. We have one Indian clergyman here now. He is one of the Indians who was captured by the soldiers, when a boy, some years ago...

...Please old friend help me out of my difficulty. Do what you can for us among your own people and send me the addresses of old college friends and any others who are likely to assist. I am the only Lampeter man who is in the heathen field; old St. David's College can do something for its representative...

Front door to Mission school, before porch was added. Standing, Left: The mailman, Dewi Roberts, Effie Jones, unidentified woman, Mrs. Roberts, & 3 daughters-Seated, left: Ivie Raynor & Elinor Roberts

Chapter 9

School Life

When the little Shoshone girls were first enrolled in the Shoshone Mission School in the 1890's and early 1900's, they found life there really difficult, strange, confining and even frightening.

"Listen, what is that loud, ringing noise, and all the girls are running!"

"Something must be chasing them!"

"I will run home to my mother!"

"Nes um-bea yn-gan-i nam-a-soo nook-it."

Then a comforting companion advises, "ka, kim, in-a dick-up. Sik gah."

"Oh, climb up on this? Is this food? I do smell beef. Eeg-it-si, nea ka dick-up. Tose-te-cup? Is it really tose-te-cup? I am a little hungry."

For a long time the children would not eat any cooked vegetables though they enjoyed going to the garden and eating raw turnips, carrots, onions and peas. Milk and butter, though served without fail at all meals, simply were not accepted as food for some time. Meanwhile, the butter was generously applied to their hair and later to the pillowslips. Even dessert was often left uneaten. But how they loved wild fruit. They would go down to the bank of Trout Creek, gather and eat gooseberries (green or ripe) currants and all the buffalo berries they could hold. They soon learned that the berries must be gathered and preserved for the winter. Then every fall, great dishpans full of boiling fruit filled the kitchen with a delicious smell.

The huge black stove in the kitchen had once been the hub of many lives. The firebox was very deep and it took hours for the oven and the stove lids to begin to get warm. I remember seeing kettles of buffalo berry jelly being stirred and cooked there. The older girls would take turns stirring this delicious red syrup. The Indian girls were eager to gather any berries and also eat as many as they gathered. The snakes in Crooked Creek Canyon always worried me a little, but the older girls didn't seem too concerned when we heard a rattler. They would soon be gone with lots of yelling and well aimed stones.

The girls would pull a huge canvas tarp close to the base of the berry bushes. With the smaller children holding the tarp around the sides, the older girls would whack the bushes and the berries, leaves, small spiders and dust would soon fill the tarp. These would be emptied into buckets and the whole process would begin again. Berry picking would usually begin in the heat of August, and the buffalo berry jelly was eaten during winter.

When we visited the Mission my grandfather always explained to us that as guests we were very welcome to eat at the Mission, but he would pay for each of our meals. His aim was to teach us that we did not eat food that was given, earned or raised for the little Indian girls. The Indians were an honest and fair people, and my grandfather taught us that they would remain so if treated honestly and fairly by us at all times. We were the minority race on the Reservation and, therefore, guests of the Indian people.

In their free time the girls played games usually of their own invention. One of their favorites was whipping a rag ball with a slim club, a willow from the creek bank, all over the pasture. In winter a similar game was played on the ice with a small stone whipped by strips of colored cloth tied to a long stick. Sometimes after school, a walk across the field and up on a hill took them to a high ridge of rocks where they had a good time "coining" money by grinding sandstone pieces. In a deep fissure in the same rocks, could be seen the blankets which wrapped the body of an Indian child buried there.

A fine pair of stilts could be made from young trees with the right kind of branches growing from the main staff. The smaller branch was cut off a few inches from the main. Willows woven between the main staff and the branch made a comfortable and safe foot rest. Wading with these stilts in the creek and in the big irrigation laterals, the beds of which were full of slippery boulders, gave them a great thrill and many a cold bath.

These little Shoshone girls also discovered that the mud around the Mission building was a good substitute for modeling clay. On a wide, sloping bank of the creek, they made a wonderful model of an Indian camp, most elaborate in detail and all in mud. There were men and women "Round-Dancing," men Wolf-Dancing, others riding and hunting, and women hanging strips of meat to dry while carrying either a baby-board or a bundle of firewood on their backs. Unfortunately, when the cattle came to drink, the village was destroyed.

Shoshone Girls Playing (Juggling Balls), Shoshone Mission

A more permanent camp was built under the apple trees in the orchard. Their small teepees made of willows and covered with pieces of white cloth were beautiful. (For the novice, a teepee is most difficult to put up.) Everyone in this camp; men, women and children, was dressed in old time Indian costumes. Horses with squaw saddles, dogs, buffalo and

Shoshone Mission Students

even the campfires were cleverly made of scraps of colored cloth and buckskin, all on clay models. These same children showed skill in another favorite game. All sat or stood in a ring. Then, with hardened mud balls made the day before, they began to sing. Keeping time with the singing, they would toss in the air and catch four or six balls in turn with seldom a miss.

Near the Mission school was a slough in which, only once, the girls were found fishing. Their bait was a young skunk tied to a long, limber willow; the fish was the same skunk, repeatedly pulled out of the water and thrown back. The game didn't last long as there was so much of interest to do before a bell would ring, calling them in.

Occasionally a game was started that was taboo. Such a game was being played once by a group of small boys. They were throwing narrow boards in the air, making a sharp, whistling noise when Wild Man, a young medicine man, rushed up to them, grabbed two boards and broke them in pieces. "Never do that! A big wind will blow down all the teepees!" That night all the teepees along Trout Creek were blown down.

For practical purposes, the matron at the school decided to cut the hair of the children entering school to shoulder length. Usually even the smallest girl had long, thick, beautiful hair. But the matron changed her mind after dealing once with the hysterical child and the irate parents. Of course the matron didn't know that cut hair or a severed finger joint was recognized by the tribes as a mark of bereavement.

A little flattering attention paid to the older school girls by the young Indian boys was a simple and inexpensive procedure. The young man, wrapped in a blanket from head to foot, walked slowly by the Mission just about dusk playing his flute. The homemade flutes were crafted of many kinds of wood, and the music, though plaintive, was beautiful.

A bolder and certainly more startling manner of courtship and perhaps one more to the young man's taste was often resorted to. At evening, just after dark, if one looked out of the window, a pair of very bright eyes would meet one's own. No identification was possible as a blanket covered all but the eyes, and those would be disguised by white, red or yellow paint. Then he was gone, running across the field with the blanket held spread out, giving him the appearance of a huge bat.

In trying another window, the same luck or better would hold. He would be back and probably with an impetuous young friend. There were other variations of the some project. The girls' matron went one night about ten o'clock to the dormitory across the hall from her own room to see if all was well. She found everyone apparently asleep—shoes at the bedside and clothes carefully hung up for the morning. Usually the students persisted in wearing their clothes to bed. How pleased the matron was! "Oh, what good little girls. I must always be as careful of their welfare as I am of my own. I will look under some of the beds to be sure." What luck! She found him under the last bed. He scrambled out, his hair bushy and frightened eyes, wide. Too bad he forgot to go out the window and down the fire escape the way he had come in. He ran down the stairs while two big girls with convenient brooms banged him on the head all the way to the front door.

How the children loved the excitement of threshing time. It was exciting to experience the noise and clouds of dust from the threshing machine with the teams of horses walking round and round supplying the power and the men shouting at the horses and at each other!

This harvest time continued for several days, from dawn until after dark when the work went on by the light of kerosene lanterns. Some of the turmoil reached the kitchen where the preparation of many meals for the threshers, White men, and Indians was taking place. A few years later as the modern machines came into use, threshing the Indians' grain on their little farms all around the Mission may have been more profitable but the interest was never as keen.

Halloween at the Mission was another special and fun time for the Indian children. I can't remember them ever having masks, but we did gather in the "playroom" for a special treat. We would sit in a large circle and Grandpapa would show us pictures with the Magic Lantern. These were pictures of old fashioned children having a skating party, or of stories from the Bible, or of illustrated poems. There was magic in these pictures with the light behind them. A light was run by kerosene or sometimes a flashlight was held up so that a picture could be reflected on a white sheet fastened up to the wall. The evening would end with refreshments for all of us, maybe half an orange with a few pieces of candy. We always attended these events at the mission because my parents helped out on these special days.

Life in a Mission boarding school was unbelievably hard.[31] It was full of new problems every day and yet, very often, these provided the most wonderful and rewarding experiences.

---

[31] *My grandparents' living quarters were stark and primitive. Their room, near the kitchen on the south side of the building, was very small. It held a double bed, a small metal bed for a visiting grandchild to stay in, a stove with a coal bucket standing near by, a washstand with a bowl and a pitcher on it, and a wardrobe against the wall. This wardrobe held all of their personal possessions. My grandfather had built a small room and a white picket fence around the outside of the door of this tiny 10 x 12 addition. This was called the playroom and was the only private place on the entire grounds for my grandmother to take her small children and have them enclosed in a small yard. There was a garden with flowers in it, some of the seeds had come from Wales and some from England. This room has been torn down, and it's hard to see where it was attached to the building.*

I remember the school was a very busy place as summer was coming to an end. When I was about ten years old I was allowed to go to the Mission and help my aunt get ready for the first days of school. The dormitories had to be prepared first. In the large room, there were about fifteen or twenty iron cots. Each bed had to be made up with clean blankets, sheets and spreads; these beds were to be made up perfectly. A bed was never finished until there was not one wrinkle in it. The bedding at the bottom of the bed was tucked in with square corners, and each spread hung exactly the same distance from the floor on each side. I was young and didn't really understand why each bed had to be perfect and all look just the same, but I soon found out that this was a given since, if the sheet was a little crooked, we would start again. There were two older Indian girls who had been trained long ago in making the smaller dormitory ready for school. They knew that you did not hurry and do a sloppy job or the whole process had to be done all over.

The next chore was a trip up the ladder to the attic. This was quite an adventure. The school capes, dresses, black shoes and warm woolen sweaters were carried down first. These had been packed in trunks and were placed carefully on the rafters so that they would not break through the plaster ceiling. The attic was a place of great treasures, records and curious locked boxes. The space was like crawling into an oven, as no insulation was used at this time. Perhaps this terrific heat had kept some of the old records preserved because no one could stay up there long enough to scatter the old papers. The ladder to the attic was near the railing around the upstairs hallway. I could peek over the ladder and clear down into the main hall of the Mission. After getting over this first dizzy spell I would try not to look over again. We finally finished carrying down the piles of clothing and arranged them on the long benches in the upstairs hallway, according to size. There was no storage place for clothing in the dormitories, just a few hooks around the room.

Then we went to the laundry room and made sure that it was clean, the towels on the wooden bench and everything ready for the girls to come and enter school.

The children came on Sunday afternoon, early enough so that each girl would have time to get her hair washed and take a bath, before marching in line to the Chapel for service at four o'clock. The girls always dressed alike and the four year old girls wore the same dress and sweater or coat style as the fourteen year old girls.

Many of the former pupils — mothers, grandmothers and great-grandmothers — now often speak with gratitude of the happy years they spent in school at the Mission. Fortunately they knew nothing of trying to operate the school on such a pittance of money. All the water, such hard water, had to be dipped in buckets from the creek after a hole had been chopped in the ice if it were winter, then carried nearly a quarter of a mile. Perhaps they do remember the lovely irrigation ditch that ran through the Mission grounds in summer, watering the orchard, shade trees and clover, and making a wonderful place to wade and play. But they may not have realized that stoves in all the rooms upstairs and down had to be kept full of wood and coal, and the bread left to rise overnight on a table by the stove, sometimes froze.

Arapahoe Ministry; Arapahoe Friends

John Roberts acted as the Episcopal missionary to the Arapahoes as well as the Shoshones, from 1883 to 1949. As he had with the Shoshones, Roberts, working with the native Arapahoe clergyman, the Rev. Sherman Coolidge, held the first services for the Arapahoes in their camps. Eventually, in 1898, services were held in a small log chapel called Our Father's House. This chapel was situated in an Arapahoe village about eight miles east of the Agency. Members of the congregation, living in camps nearby, would watch for the clergyman's buckboard and team and then they would start walking across the prairie toward the chapel.

Arapahoe translations of parts of the bible, parts of the Book of Common Prayer and a Catechism, were used in the services. The congregation sometimes numbered over two hundred. Then the little log chapel was too small and they would assemble in the Tribal Council House. In this primitive structure, which afforded poor protection from the weather, they knelt on the damp earth floor to receive the Holy Communion.

Both Arapahoe and Shoshone children had attended school at the Shoshone Indian Agency in the small building called the "Mission House" which had served for the service Bishop Randall had conducted in 1873 and in which held services until the Church of the Redeemer was built in 1884.

At an early service where Herbert Welsh, the catechist, presented sixteen candidates for Baptism, of whom eleven were adults, Roberts wrote that:

> The majority were former pupils of mine in the old [first] Government School at the Agency on the banks of Trout Creek. Two of them, John Lone Man and Carey Shot Gun, middle-aged men, came up in the presence of the company of their own free will and accord, sought and received the sacrament of Baptism. All the prominent men present were old pupils: Yellow Calf, William Penn, Seth Willow, Ned Wanstall, Henry Lee, Adam Redman, Walter White Owl, Herbert Welsh, and a long train of others of the younger generation, many of them now with families of their own.

Our Father's House after removal from original site (1 mile distance)
Current site is at Saint Michael's Mission

In speaking of this time, Father Roberts added, "For want of a better, I acted as organist while the men sang lustily some of the hymns which they had learned long ago in school. They asked for them invariably because they reminded them of the good old days and playmates that were gone." Many of the young Arapahoe boys that came to the government school, untutored and knowing only the free camp life, grew to be remarkably fine men. Many did excellent work as catechists in the church, others were wise leaders in their tribe. These former pupils of Rev. John Roberts came directly under his influence every day as he was their school superintendent, teacher and clergyman. After they left school they often came to him for advice and counsel.

Fremont Arthur was the first Arapahoe catechist to assist with a church service. The Arapahoe translation of the service was used by the priest, the catechist and the native congregation for some years, until English was commonly spoken. For his services, the church paid Fremont a scanty pittance but with it and the little he made by working his ranch, he managed to keep his family and to help a horde of hungry relatives. He went on giving with both hands to all who asked, teaching and preaching Jesus Christ and the Resurrection to all his people. As a raise in pay, he was at one time offered a government job but he declined the offer, saying he would rather remain where he was and do what he could for those around him. Enough cannot be said for this faithful and consecrated young man. His people had lost in the insatiable encroachment of civilization,``` not only their old life and haunts but also their old beliefs.

Fremont Arthur, age thirty years, died on St. Barnabas Day, 1901, of pneumonia brought on by exposure. In his death, the Arapahoes suffered a great loss. His zeal in making known the truths of the Gospel, was untiring, uncompromising in spite of much bitterness stirred up against him. Two days before his death, he made an address to the young people at the school. His subject was, "The Life Everlasting, Je-thau-je-nee." During that week and the following, one hundred and seven pupils, Arapahoes and Shoshones, asked for and received the Sacrament of Baptism. Now that tongue is silent, and his people who, as a rule are of a thoughtful turn of mind, will perhaps, remember his words. Fremont served as a sergeant in the Indian Company, U.S. Army, for three years, at Fort Washakie. His grave is in the St. Michael's cemetery. On the headstone was this inscription, [now entirely obliterated] written by his friend Michael White Hawk:

Fremont Arthur, Faithful Evangelist to his people, the Arapahoe Indians.

Jae-da-a-he-de [Large Man] Died 1901, age 30 years

Ne-dawn He-ja-va, He-nau-nau-a-nau- the-da-he Ne-au-saun

[The first Arapahoe preacher of the Son of the Unknown on High]

Michael White Hawk, another Arapahoe evangelist, took Fremont Arthur's place as catechist, after Fremont's death. This is White Hawk's story written by the hand of Rev. John Roberts, in 1907:

> Thirty five years ago, in the Big Horn Mountains in Wyoming, a little Arapaho Indian boy was born. The teepee that sheltered him was pitched with others in a beautiful valley, in which game and fish were plentiful and in their season, berries and roots. The Arapahoes, being expert hunters, supplied plenty of good things to eat at the camp fires. They had plenty of buckskin and pelts to wear and hides to make teepees with. One might suppose that this little Indian boy had a happy place to live in but it was not so, for in addition to many other dangers, there was the constant peril of an attack from hostile Indians. Brave and wary as the Arapahoes were, many a time when the camps raided, their men killed and their women and children carried off by enemies to other tribes, so that it was a fortunate thing for them when in 1878 the United States Government compelled them to give up their roving life in the hunting ground to settle down on the Shoshone Reservation under the protection of the soldiers at Fort Washakie.
>
> The little boy was about six years old when he came to live on the Reservation. Being a bright thoughtful lad, the medicine men took pride in teaching him the past history of the Arapahoes and their ancient lore.
>
> The sacred order among them, similar to the Levites of the Jews or the Druids of the Celts, has preserved a wonderful store of traditions which reach back far into the past.
>
> Through this Secret Society, he learned that long, long ago, in coming to this "new earth" from the "old earth," his people crossed over on ice somewhere in the far North; that while they were crossing the ice broke up and the greater part

of the tribe was drowned; that those who had not reached the water returned whence they came, and those who had landed on this side, after bewailing their loss, continued their journey, traveling toward the South — the Arapahoes call the south, "down below" — the north, "to windward."

They had with them dogs and elk (reindeer) and so they came on down. They saw for the first time, "dark animals" (deer), "noisy animals" (their name for buffalo) and "big horns" (mountain sheep). By and by they found other people who had preceded them. These lived in grass lodges and ate snakes and walked with a shuffling gait peculiar to themselves. To these they gave the name of "Snake Indians" or "those who live in grass wigwams." Later they found other people who have now all passed away. These lived in the rocks and canyons. They were very short of stature, not taller than children but they were very strong and powerfully built. They named these "little catchers" for they would trail an Arapahoe and when they had caught him, they would kill him with the flint-pointed arrows and carry him off to feast on, for they were cannibals.

Many strange tales did they tell him of these aboriginal, pygmies, which goes to show that they were human beings of a very low type.

Then the old men, the "Janajehenan" told this boy of many ancient customs and ceremonies. Among them were these: that seven was a mystic number, that it had been the custom to pluck off the shoe as a pledge, that the feet must be uncovered when on holy ground, that at the severe illness of a son, a piece of the skin of the forearm must be offered to the four watchers that stand at the four quarters of the earth; that offerings must be made, with fasting and prayer, upon altars of stone, on the high places, to the powers of the air; that prayer is most efficacious with the burning of incense; that before crossing a swollen stream propitiatory offerings must be made to the fish-god who caused the drowning of so many of their people; that in drinking at a stream, the water should be lapped with the hand (in a most peculiar manner) like a dog lappeth with his tongue.

Then, too, these old men taught him the religion of their forefathers, as it had been handed down to them. They told him of the si-eja-the, "flat-pipe" which was given to the first Arapahoe by "Jevaneauthau," the Strange Being on High and that he must regard that pipe with awe as being most holy, for it had led the people in their pilgrimage through the ages. In the place where it abode, there they pitched their tents, when it moved on, they journeyed. That pipe, was the "hodde Jevaneauthau," the Chariot of God, for it carried the spirits (shades) of dying Arapahoes to "Our Home." That at all times, even to this day, that pipe worked wondrously. They told him that the Arapahoes were the first created of all peoples, that for them, this earth was formed. They told him the story of the creation, that in the beginning this earth was covered by the waters of a flood, except the top-most peak of a high mountain. On it sat the first Arapahoe, weeping. Looking up he saw Jevaneauthau coming to him walking on the water. Being asked why he wept, the Arapahoe replied that he was lonely and homeless. Jevaneauthau then commanded a dove to find a country for the Arapahoe. Returning after a fruitless search, the dove said, "The water is over all." A turtle was then bidden on the same errand. It at once dived into the water and brought up some mud in its mouth and said, "The earth is under the water." Jevaneauthau then said, "Let the waters flow away to the big seas and let the dry land appear." Immediately a beautiful vision of mountains and valleys, hills and plains appeared before them, fresh and green as in spring. All this was for the Arapahoe and his descendants forever. Then, while walking in this beautiful place, Jevaneauthau threw some pebbles in a deep lake. Seeing them sink into the depths, the Arapahoe cried, "Oh, are my children to die?" To comfort him, Jevaneauthau handed to him the flat-pipe and said to him, "Treasure this most carefully, for it will be to your children, during life, a guide and a blessing. When they die, it will carry their souls safe to 'Our Home' and when it wastes away, their dead bodies will rise again. With the great hosts of the dead, I, the Deliverer, will come from the West to be Chief over my people forever. Be kind to your friends. Fight bravely your enemies. Farewell."

Knowing the Arapahoe stories, Michael, as a young man stood watching the Indian pupils harvesting the school grain. Seeing a gap in the line of workers, he threw off his blanket and unbidden, worked until the evening. At supper, a suit of clothes was given him, his scalp lock and long black braids were clipped off by one of the other boys and he was enrolled as Michael, it being St. Michael's and All Angels Day.

He was an apt pupil but it was a long time before he would make use of the White man's language or accept his religion. Under the instruction of his clergyman and of his fellow pupil, Fremont Arthur and others, he at length believed and became a Christian. He received Holy Baptism and in due time was confirmed and became a Communicant. He thinks that in the religion of his forefathers, the truths of god can be traced and believes that their Jevaneauthau is Jehovah and that they in their long wandering have lost the truth. Anxious that his people should have the Word of God in their own tongue, he has with great pains and care, helped with the translation of the Gospel of St. Luke into Arapahoe. Last summer, on the untimely death of Fremont Arthur, the native evangelist saw the gap in the harvest field. Michael, again unbidden, stepped forward into his friend's place and worked faithfully as a catechist until his death from tuberculosis in 1907.

White Hawk was a great help to the Rev. John Roberts in the work of translating the Gospel of St. Luke into the Arapahoe language. Such translation was very difficult since the Arapahoe language, like the Shoshone, is an unwritten one.

Herbert Welsh then took up the work that Michael White hawk had done so well. Herbert helped Mr. Roberts with the revision of some of the Arapahoe translations which he had made during the years 1895-1902. some of these manuscripts, the Order of Confirmation, the form of Solemnization of Matrimony, the Visitation of the Sick and the Service of the Burial of the Dead, were never printed for lack of funds.

Herbert worked not only for the spiritual welfare of his people but he did all he could to encourage them to farm their allotments and to build homes for themselves. He fenced in and cultivated a productive homestead on which he raised crops of grain, hay and garden vegetables. Someone asked Herbert how much Mr. Roberts paid him for his work. When he said the amount, the comment was, "That's pretty poor pay." "Well," said Herbert, "It's pretty poor preach."

Josiah Oldman, an Arapahoe of a little later time, was a catechist, lay reader and interpreter at St. Michael's Mission for fifteen years. He died in 1939 at the age of sixty years.

Tom Crispin was another Arapahoe boy who grew up to fill the office of Catechist in the work of the church. He arrived at the Reservation on St. Crispin's Day and was so named by Dr. Roberts. He died at his sheep camp when he was sixty years old. Those who have been longer in the missionary field realize as others seldom do, how important is the help of native workers among their own people.

There were many other outstanding young men among the Arapahoes beside those already named. There was Black Coal, Tab-be-tha-the, (Shot-off-fingers) the last chief of the Northern Arapahoes. John Roberts had this to say about this remarkable man:

> Black Coal was my friend. I could never have established the government school of 1884 without Black Coal's help. This man deserves the name of the unsung hero. He was always the staunch supporter of the government, and accompanied several of the expeditions of the United States troops against the hostile Sioux and Cheyenne. He was shot through the chest at the Bates Battle in 1874, two fingers were also shot off. He was a contemporary of Chief Washakie and a peer of that chief. Black Coal was more than chief of the Arapahoes. The Arapahoes elected him chief of their tribe. His word was not law except it coincided with the will of his people. He was brave, calm and magnanimous, a fine big man. He would talk to a two year old child with the same attention and respect as he would to an adult. He was honorable; if he borrowed money, he always paid it back.

The celebrated Sioux Chief Red Cloud attempted, unsuccessfully, to induce Black Coal, with his band, to join him at Red Cloud Agency as allies of the Sioux Cheyennes, to overwhelm the hated Whites. Black Coal told him that he would rather be Chief of the Arapahoes then the sub-chief to Red Cloud.

When John Roberts was once asked if Black Coal was a Christian, he replied, "I don't know what you mean. He was very religious, the religion of the Hebrews. He looked forward to the Coming, as all of the Arapahoes did, of the Promised Great one - looking for a Messiah they called God."

Black Coal, an Arapahoe Chief and friend of Mr. Roberts

Of Sumner Black Coal, his adopted son, Roberts writes, "I have great hopes in the success of Sumner's work among his people and sincerely trust that his services can be permanently secured."

Those Arapahoes who made so many raids against the Whites in Wyoming, were renegades from Black Coal's band, young men who joined the Sioux and Cheyennes who were enemies of the White people. The action of these marauders brought disrepute upon the whole Arapahoe tribe. So historians have ignored the undoubted services of Black Coal. Dr. Roberts describes him as a man of unusual stature and strength, of superior intelligence and sterling worth. He was a very religious man. Black Coal died in July 1893, at the age of fifty years. He was buried in the tribal cemetery of the lower Arapahoes, about eighteen miles east of Fort Washakie and perhaps five miles north of Arapahoe. His grave is marked by a sandstone obelisk erected by his tribe. It bears the following inscription;

> Black coal, chief of the Northern Arapahoes
> Died July 10, 1893, age fifty years,
> Erected by the Northern Arapahoes
> In honor of a Brave and Honest Man

Young Chief, a brother of Black Coal, was as reliable and honorable as anyone could be. He was always to be found, with his quiet and unassuming manner, at his post as door-keeper at the warehouse, when rations were given out to the Indians. At Young Chief's death, Black Coal adopted his boy, Sumner, as his own. Sumner was a fine and intelligent young man. His quick action and clear thinking prevented a wreck on the North Western passenger train at a time when heavy rains had caused the Muskrat Creek to overflow its banks and wash out the pilings of the bridge. Sumner was walking home from Shoshoni when he found the break. He built a fire on the tracks and stopped the train without a minute to spare. By his prompt action he saved many lives and much property.

Sharp Nose, Wau-gu-a, meaning "plume" was the last war chief of the Northern Arapahoes. Enlisted scout of the United States Army, his discharge reads, "Sharp Nose, sergeant Indian scout, enrolled October, 1876, to serve three months; discharged January, 1877, at Camp Robinson, Nebraska. Signed W.P. Clark, Lieut., 2nd. Cavalry, Commanding Scouts." His endorsement of Sharp Nose read: "Keen-eyed, brave, intelligent, trust worthy, with very superior judgment; an efficient guide and enlisted scout; gave reliable information with regard to location of village and topography of adjacent country and rendered distinguished service with hostile Cheyennes on November, 1876."

Lieut. Clark accompanied President Arthur when he passed through the Reservation on his way to the Yellowstone Park in August 1883. Lieut. Clark published the standard book on the Indian Sign Language. Sharp Nose was his instructor. [A later book was the "*Universal American Indian Sign Language*" by William Tomkins. First edition 1926.] Sharp Nose died in June 1901 and was buried "in the rocks" by his own people.

Sam Shot Gun, better known as Jabo, was also a scout. He was with Gen. Crook in 1876. Jabo died November 5, 1941, at the age of ninety years.

Of Little Wolf, an Arapahoe medicine man, Roberts wrote he, "is always a very attentive listener to the Story of the Gospel and often repeats what I say to those present. I should like very much to have some illustrations of the ministry and life of our hut about 30 feet long and 20 feet wide. It is a general rendezvous of the head men, council room, medicine lodge and hospital. Little Wolf is a doctor of great renown among his people, and indeed the old gentleman is very successful in his treatment and charges two or three ponies for cure."

Little Wolf charged nothing when he failed. Most of his patients were very poor and these he treated gratuitously. Little Wolf claimed he held a written communication which endowed him with supernatural powers from above and which he got in a wonderful way. One bright, starry night as he lay in his lodge, he heard his name called, "Gan-hau-cutch-a!" This sent him out of his bed and out of doors. Looking up, he saw a document floating in the air above his teepee. Not being encumbered with clothing, he ran up the side of the teepee and stood on the end of a teepee pole and snatched the "wath-thou-nah-ha," the writing. He had secured for himself the "bed-den," the power. He said he had the document somewhere, in safe keeping, but no one seems to have seen it. While telling the missionary more wondrous tales than this, he would tremble with excitement.

Yellow Calf, sometimes spoken of as George Caldwell, was a strong leader among the members of the tribe and a progressive leader. He gave five acres of his allotment of land for the site of one of the Mission churches. At one of the services held at his camp two hundred and fifty persons

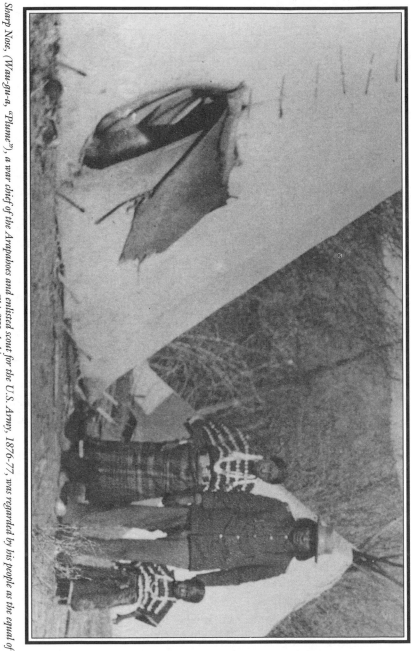

Sharp Nose, (Wau-gu-a, "Plume"), a war chief of the Arapahoes and enlisted scout for the U.S. Army, 1876-77, was regarded by his people as the equal of Chief Washakie.

assembled. An account of the Christmas service held for the Arapahoes before the Mission was established, was dictated to Alice Beath by John Roberts about 1912. The date is not confirmed but would probably be after Christmas 1912:

> Sunday, December 29, was a day of eager anticipation by the Arapahoes, for on that afternoon, Mr. Roberts had a Christmas service in the Arapahoe Council House, the Church being too small to accommodate the crowd. The Indians camped along the river and as the hour for the service approached, Seth-will, the crier, bade them all come, and 250 Arapahoes came — men, women and children — clad in their best in honor of the occasion. The men were seated on one side of the hall, the women and children on the opposite side. Yellow Calf gave a short talk and spoke of the great kindness of their Eastern friends to the Arapahoes, and how much the Indians should appreciate this interest. He concluded by congratulating them that a new Mission is about to be established by the Bishop [Thomas]. Then Mr. Roberts gave an interesting talk on the joys of the Christmas Season, after which he administered the Sacrament of Baptism to the following: Thomas Friday, John Brown, Vernon Wolf-Arrows, Benjamin White Plume, Lone Bull Grasshopper, Lone Kills Whiteplume, Red Woman White, Joseph Porcupine, Plenty Ear-rings Mountain Sheep, Sings Across, Sharp Nose.
>
> After prayers and the blessing, the gifts were distributed by Herbert Welsh and Tom Crispin, catechists. Each person was remembered. The men received woolen shirts, the women cloth for dresses.

When Rev. Roberts built St. Michael's Mission, this small chapel was moved [in 1919] from Yellow Calf's Camp to the land he had given to found the Mission. It has been considerably enlarged since then. St. Michael's, originally a boarding school, was later converted to a day school and used as such until the Mill Creek School was built. Yellow Calf died on December 15, 1938, at the age of 76. He was a good friend to Roberts.

Just as with the Shoshones, it was a good many years before the Arapahoe women would work in the homes of the White people. There

Yellow Calf, the Arapahoe Chief who provided the original land for our Father's House at St. Michael's Mission

were exceptions. In the missionary clergyman's first home, which was two small rooms built on the east end of the Church of the Redeemer (before the Shoshone Mission was built and not even plastered on account of a lack of funds) there were three Arapahoe women who helped, at different times, with the care of the Roberts children. How kind and faithful they were; Pretty, Old Woods and Walking Crow.[32] From this close association of the children with their nurse maid, one of the little girls spoke Arapahoe before she learned to speak English. These Arapahoe women must have had something of the Spartan in their makeup as shown by the custom of their daily bath and shampoo in the icy water of Trout Creek.

These were just a few of the fine Arapahoe people who were friends of John Roberts and helped him in his work.

---

[32] *Walking Crow was Elinor Roberts' nursemaid and taught her the Arapahoe language, which Elinor spoke fluently the rest of her life.*

St. Michaels - The Arapahoe Episcopal Mission

John Roberts' cherished hope that the Arapahoes would also have their own Mission, was finally realized in 1917. Many Arapahoe men, former pupils of the Rev. John Roberts, were of the greatest help in establishing this. They felt it was their own. Some of their leaders rose up during a council meeting and said, "We know that this school is to go on for the Arapahoe people through all the years. It is not for our children only but for their children and their children's children."

St. Michael's was named in honor of Michael White Hawk, the Arapahoe who helped with the translation of the Gospels, the Lord's Prayer and the Creed into his own language. In a letter from John Roberts printed in the *The Bible Society Record, 1904*, he quotes Michael White Hawk concerning the Indians statement that the truth of God could be dimly traced in the religion of his forefathers.

Roberts also had help in raising enough money from outside the Reservation for the Arapahoe Mission. The following letter written by the Arapahoe priest Sherman Coolidge to the Rt. Rev. John F. Spalding, D.D., the presiding bishop in 1885, shows Coolidge's fervent desire to help in getting the Arapahoe Mission established:

April 23, 1885

Rt. Rev. John F. Spalding, D.D.
My Dear Bishop:

...My chief work during the past quarter has been in aiding the school work at the Agency, teaching in the Arapahoe department of the school. I find that the Arapahoe and Shoshone children are docile and intelligent, as I have found Indian children to be among the Ojibways, the Santee, Sisseton and Yankton Sioux and other tribes, and they learn very willingly and readily. Notwithstanding that this Wind River School is only two years old, I believe it is doing as much good as any other institution of its kind in the U.S. and that the Superintendent, Rev. John Roberts, and his co-workers deserve any and every help which the church, as well as the government, can give them, and I doubt whether those who are doing its work and bearing its burdens can fully realize what they are doing for these poor [people], their country and the Christian religion.

I have held services and preached at Fort Washakie and Lander every other Sunday, and delivered one sermon at the Agency. I have also buried one Indian and visited about twenty-five teepees. I have succeeded to obtain the promise of three of the Arapahoes to commence farming, and to continue until they have secured a home for themselves and their families. I am very desirous to raise a fund now to the amount of six or seven hundred dollars with which to build a Mission House to be situated at my Uncle Sharp Nose's camp, about ten or twelve miles from here, and where I understand you wish to locate a Chapel. If we establish a permanent Mission there, I think many Arapahoes will settle around and near it. The Sioux or Dakotah language is said to be one of the easiest of Indian languages to learn, and the Arapahoe one of the hardest. I studied the Sioux languages for six months, yet I have acquired more Arapahoe in the same length of time than I did the Dakotah. I have no difficulty in the pronunciation at all. I do not think it will take as long to learn my native tongue as it would a new one, however casy.

I know of no state or territory where the Church has a more glorious field as man's educator, "intellectual, as well as spiritual," than she has in this, her new Missionary Jurisdiction of Wyoming Territory, and more especially on the Reservation where the need of civilization is so imperious, and where people are willing, so favorably, for the reception of the Gospel story of the love of God.

I am sincerely yours,
Sherman Coolidge, Native Missionary to the Arapahoes

In 1910, Mrs. Baird Cooper of Philadelphia, Pennsylvania, became interested in missionary work, through Bishop Nathaniel S. Thomas, then bishop of Wyoming. She came west to the Wind River Reservation and spent several summers at the Shoshone Indian Mission. After seeing the work being done there, she felt a Mission school for the Arapahoes would be of the greatest benefit to them. She decided to give all her time and money toward that purpose.

After studying the necessary facts and collecting many pictures of Indians and Indian life, Mrs. Cooper returned to her home in Philadelphia. By lecturing and showing her Indian pictures in many Eastern cities, she raised enough money — counting in the gift of her personal wealth — to put up several of the buildings of the St. Michael's Mission. She continued her work for several years. Everything she collected was used for the Mission. Her plan was for a school, a center for teaching of the Christian religion. The academic studies would follow the required course in the district schools.

Mrs. Baird Cooper, St. Michael's Benefactor, taken in N.Y.C.

In 1936 or 1937, Mrs. Sherman Coolidge made a gift to St. Michael's of $7,000.00. Mrs. Cooper's and Mrs. Coolidge's gifts are two of the many generous grants that made St. Michael's financially substantial. St. Michael's Mission has enjoyed comfortable financial circumstances throughout the years by the generous endowment of Mrs. Baird Cooper of approximately $30,000 to $40,000, according to the Convocational Journal of the Missionary District of Wyoming in 1913. Additionally, from that same Journal in 1921, the convocational sermon recorded said, "There are, in wills known to me, sums which will go into the endowment of St. Michael's Mission, amounting to $60,000."

The great difference that a boarding school can make was well marked between the little children who entered the Shoshone Mission School directly from the camps in 1890, and the children who entered St. Michael's in 1917. The pupils enrolling at St. Michael's were, in a great degree, familiar with their new surroundings as most of their mothers and fathers had attended the government boarding school.

There were 150 to 200 Arapahoe girls and boys who made the Mission their home. The buildings of the Mission were placed in a circle. Included in the circle were the church, Our Father's House, which had been moved to the Mission grounds from Yellow Calf's camp and enlarged; the boys' two-story dormitory and dining room; the two-story school building and several cottages. In each cottage a group of girls lived and learned to keep house under the direction of and with the help of a house mother. Usually an Episcopal clergyman was at the head of the Mission. A staff of teachers and a nurse, highly educated in their professions, worked under the clergyman.

The boarding schools have done a most telling work, surely and steadily, to change the lives of the Indian people for the better.[33] In the church boarding schools especially, their instruction could not well be improved. Almost all of the young people have been baptized and confirmed. Most of the old people are no longer wandering nomads. They have now settled down to a quiet, industrious life on their farms and allotments where they earn their living. The influence of the Shoshone Mission has greatly prospered the work of the church among the Shoshones. Each year at the time of the Bishop's visitation, a class of girls is presented for Confirmation at the chapel of the Holy Saints John.

---

[33] *Grandpapa worked among the Arapahoe Indians for as many years as he was able to travel to their part of the Reservation. When I was quite young, I remember him stopping at our home in Fort Washakie in his small buggy. He was on his way to St. Michael's and had stopped to see if we would like to drive down with him. My mother sat in front with him, my sister and I on the small box behind the buggy seat. As we drove past the Hot Springs, I can remember the sound of the pony's hoofs on the road. It sounded hollow, as if there were a large cavity in the earth underneath. We stopped and looked at Sherman Coolidge's land bordering the Little Wind River and the acres that my grandfather owned, called "Yellow Bears," on the east side of the Coolidge property.*

St. Michael's Mission was an interesting place to visit. There were large two-story dormitories with big round tubes outside for evacuation in case of fire. If school was not in session, we would climb up the stairs, then use these "fire escapes" for a wild and exciting ride to the ground below.

The Arapahoe children would stand and look at us. We had little understanding of the Arapahoe language so they could talk about us freely as we stood and looked at them. A few miles from Fort Washakie had put us into another culture. The Arapahoes and the Shoshones neither looked nor spoke alike.

Four boarding schools were built on the Reservation for the two tribes. In a letter dated 1884, John Roberts states, "The Roman Catholics are establishing a mission thirty miles below the Shoshone Agency and the buildings are going up now." Five years later he wrote, "The Roman Catholics have come and are working successfully. The Indians are surrounded by Christianity." The Government Boarding School, built in 1892, at the site of the present day Fort Washakie school, had both Shoshone and Arapahoe students and eventually some from tribes outside the state. For a while, Roberts held services and classes for this school as well.

Chapter 12

Summing up the Reservation Work

The work on the Reservation from 1883 through the nineties was slow; in a report made in the early 1900's, Mr. Roberts writes:

Some of the Indians now live in log cabins and some still prefer the old time teepee. In winter they put up a wind break of poles and brush. They try to camp in some sheltered nook by a grove of trees. There is very little furniture in the ordinary teepee. Along the inside, on the ground, are laid some twigs and rushes over which old quilts and blankets are thrown. These are seats during the day and beds at night. By the opening, which serves as a door, cooking utensils are kept: a black kettle, a frying pan and a coffee boiler, a bucket of water and some tin plates and cups. Behind these are stored the little stock of groceries - coffee, sugar, some flour and perhaps a can of baking powder. The supply of meat is kept outdoors, hung out of reach of any animals. The Indians have no regular time for meals. The women cook when the men are hungry — except supper time, especially in winter, is a fixed affair. A bright fire lights up the teepee so that it looks, to a passer-by, in the darkness, like a very inviting place to stop. Grouped around the fire are Indian warriors, probably cold and hungry having recently returned from the hunt.

From John Roberts' Journal

By 1900 a letter, written by Rev. John Roberts to Bishop James B. Funsten reads:

My dear Bishop:

The church work has progressed steadily though slowly. Services have been held in the Shoshone Church, the Chapel of the Holy Saints John, in the Arapahoe Church, our Father's House, and at central points in the Indian camps. The services at the Church of the Redeemer, at Shoshone Agency, have been well attended by government men and by soldiers at the Fort.

The Arapahoe catechist, Fremont Arthur, has been very faithful in his duties and has worked bravely among his people in the face of strong opposition on the part of the medicine men and others. The service is conducted in the Arapahoe tongue, in which translation he had helped.

The Shoshone Mission has been prosperous during the year past except financially. The pupils have made satisfactory progress in their school work and in their industrial training. They use the English language with reluctance and in other ways show a strong cultural prejudice.

One reason there seemed to be very little progress made in the work on the Reservation, was owing to the reticent and superstitious nature of the Indians. Yet Father Roberts labored on, steadily and quietly, often exposing himself to real dangers for there were "perils by night and perils by day." Disappointments were many. Only a man of complete dedication to his work would have undertaken such a task, a great task which was to endure sixty-six years. Then gradually and almost imperceptibly, as time and work went on, there was the beginning of a change.

In 1888, at the Pan-Anglican conference, in London, Bishop Talbot, the missionary bishop of Wyoming and Idaho, gave an interesting talk on the Indian work in Wyoming. He devoted much time to Mr. Roberts' life among the Indians. He spoke of him in the highest terms and said:

A man more devoted to his work cannot be found in the whole Anglican Church today. Mr. Roberts is a man of culture, a man of apostolic devotion. He is doing a work worthy of the past heroes of the Church utterly unconscious of doing anything great. His name will live on as founder of the Church and the pioneer of the faith in these religions. He holds a very unique place in the hearts and affections of the people of Wyoming. He is known from one end to the other of that great state, for there is scarcely a place where, at one time or another, he has not gone to lend the ever helping hand to those in trouble or distress. He is endowed with the Christian principle of self-forgetfulness and is, at all times the quiet, gracious gentleman. Distinguished people all over the state do him honor. Such pioneering as John Roberts has exemplified can never be duplicated in Wyoming. The volumes that can be written of such a life! No one can know the joys and comfort such as example has brought to many people, of the encouraging words, to carry on in the face of seeming insurmountable difficulties. We, of Wyoming, are proud that Mr. Roberts is held in such affection and we trust he will be spared many more years to carry on his heroic work for the Redman who call him "Elder Brother."

The following report, favorable from the secular point of view, was made by the Board of Indian Commissioners (F.F. Sterling, J.W. Meldrum and N.B. Crump) in 1893.

That these Indians will work if the proper influence is brought to bear, and that the land will yield abundant returns, is a fact that has been demonstrated by Rev. John Roberts in charge of the Episcopal Mission in the Shoshone Reservation.

He has one hundred and sixty acres of land upon which is located the Mission School building, a creditable two story structure enclosed by a wire and pole fence, all under cultivation and thoroughly irrigated. Mr. Roberts should be encouraged and assisted in his good work, it being a fact that cannot be successfully contradicted that he has done more toward advancing these Indians in education, farming and mechanical pursuits than all other agencies...

Signed, Frank Pierce,
Acting Secretary

One of Mr. Robert's greatest assets in dealing with the Indians, was his true statesmanship. He always held the respect of both the Indians and of government officials. In the Department of the Interior, he was considered the outstanding authority in the United States on the traditions and customs of the Shoshone and Arapahoe Indians. With his great modesty, he gave the credit of what had been accomplished, to others. His strong, kindly personality influenced many to participate in religious worship.

Chapter 13

On the Road; Ministry of the White Settlements

Rev. Roberts, traveling on horseback and later with his team and buckboard, working with and ministering to the two tribes and White settlers both on the Reservation and beyond its limits, covered a territory the size of an empire. Beside the regular services held at so many stations, usually many miles apart, there were baptisms, weddings and funeral services to take him far from the beaten path. On these longer trips, there often was a coffee pot and a couple of blankets in the back of the buckboard which lent a cheery note to the endless miles.

From Shoshone Agency, later Wind River, Roberts drove seventy miles northwest to Dubois where he held services at a ranch home, school house or some other "suitable and convenient place," before he built St. Thomas' Church. A letter written in September 26, 1907, tells of this church's beginnings:

> Dear Dr. Worcester...You will be glad to know that the encouragement you...gave...during your brief visit, has been...setting them to work to build a Church for themselves this Fall. The building will be but a modest little structure, 16 x 32 ft., but we hope to make it churchly in appearance and comfortable, rustic in style, something like our Chapel here, a Kodak view of which I mail you. I want an open roof if we can afford it, nice furniture. They have subscribed $200 at Dubois and the bishop promises $100 more, so that the building of a five or six hundred dollar church is assured...Many clergyman pass through Dubois in the summer months, to travel to the Park or visit the area's dude ranches, so they could have services there quite often with Sunday School held regularly.

Roberts also held services at Circle and at Crowheart. Circle was a small post office settlement located approximately 11 miles east of Dubois, on the east fork of Wind River. At Crowheart, in 1932, the small sum of $35.00 was collected toward the building, a few years later, of St. Ellen's Church. Toward the northeast, a little over ninety miles from Shoshone Agency was Trinity Church of Thermopolis. Intervening stations, where services were held, were St. Luke's in Shoshoni, St. James' in Riverton, St. Matthew's in Hudson, Trinity Church in Lander and St. Paul's in Milford. Services were also held from time to time at Lyons Valley, in the home of Mr. and Mrs. Robert Hall; and Sunday School, conducted by Mrs. Hall, was held in their home regularly.

The following sentences are quoted from two or three letters of Robert's concerning the beginning of Trinity Church in Thermopolis. One, dated August 1905, is addressed to a lady in that town:

I have been told of the deep interest and earnest efforts, in behalf of the church, of you good ladies of Thermopolis. Bishop Funsten has asked me to go there as often as practicable and to do what I can to assist you in establishing the new parish.

Again, in 1907, Rev. Roberts writes:

The information you gave me is very encouraging. The number of communicants has increased considerably. The church can now be established with greater hope than ever. At the convocation next month, I will be more than glad to report to the Bishop, the growing strength of Trinity Church in Thermopolis. I hope to come over next Saturday and hold the service on Sunday...I thank you and the other ladies of the guild most sincerely for the check you sent for defraying the Bishop's expenses while he was in Thermopolis. I wish also to congratulate the guild on its splendid success in raising funds for the church.

In a letter to Bishop Funsten dated 1906, Rev. Roberts writes about the beginnings of St. Luke's in Shoshoni,

Dear Bishop Funsten: I am writing you of the kind reception accorded me in Shoshoni. Two lots are offered as a site for the church, both good places to build. ...The Bishop's Committee has been elected, a Sunday School and a Ladies' Guild have been organized. A request was made by some of the people that the church would be named St. Luke's after their home church in Evanston, Illinois. The only available building for the service was the combined town hall and jail which the mayor and city council made ready and placed at our disposal. All the saloons in the town were closed during the service. The town is one of tents, iron buildings, frame and log structures and a few large buildings of imported lumber.

As soon as I hear from you I will drive down to Shoshoni again and go on from there to Thermopolis which is only thirty-two miles farther on, a matter of five or six hours with my team.

St. James' Church in Riverton was built in the fall of 1906. The Church Building Fund, along with personal contributions, aided Rev. Roberts with the financing of the building. For years Rev. John Roberts drove from Wind River to Riverton to hold the church services. The old dirt road which followed the Little Wind most of the way down the valley was a long one of between thirty-five and forty miles. With a team and buckboard, it was a day's drive. Many times he experienced Wyoming's extreme temperatures; the blazing heat of summer and the freezing cold of winter snow storms. In the later years a number of clergymen were stationed at Riverton, usually for short periods of time.

As the church building was not used every Sunday by its own congregation, it was offered for the use of other Christian denominations. In time the city outgrew the old building and a much larger and finer one took its place. Many gifts to the church have helped to beautify its interior. St. James is a strong organization and it will doubtless grow with the city in which it is so fortunately situated.

St. Matthew's church in Hudson, was built about 1909. Here, the cost of building the church was borne by the people of the town and vicinity. The people's contribution and a gift from the American Building Fund of $100.00 were for the special purpose of building a house of worship of the Episcopal Church. The site was given to the bishop and successors in office forever. Again, the Bishop's Committee gladly allowed the use of it, for divine service, to any duly ordained minister or any recognized Christian church. An excellent Church School was organized and the services were well attended.

"I have most grateful remembrances of the generosity and goodness of the people of Hudson," Roberts wrote. "It was one of the most responsive missions with which I have ever been connected."

Although he was stationed at Shoshone Agency, Rev. Roberts was very anxious to establish a Mission at Lander, a little frontier town seventeen miles from the agency.[34] The first regular church services in

---

[34] *The first Episcopal service was held in Lander in 1872. The Rt. Rev. George Maxwell Randall, Bishop of Colorado, Wyoming, New Mexico and adjacent territories, held service for the few settlers in the valley in that year and again on August 20, 1873.*

He preached to them. This was the last act of his ministry, for the hardships and exposure of the long overland journey, to and from, through what was then a region harassed by hostile Indians, caused the aged Prelate's death. His successor, Bishop J.F. Spalding, continued to make his periodic visitations to these valleys, the Reservation and Lander and on August 26, 1883, organized the Episcopal Mission here. For some time the Episcopalians worshiped in a hall placed at their disposal for that purpose by the late Maj. M.N. Baldwin. In 1885 the present Church was erected by the people at a cost of about $2,500.00. The site, like those of the Roman Catholic and Methodist churches, was donated by the most worthy gentlemen who composed the Lander Townsite committee, Mr. P.P. Dickinson, Mr. E. Amoretti and Mr. Frank Lowe. The Church services were held by the missionary priest stationed on the Indian Reservation most of the time.

Trinity Church is in a prosperous condition and will this year [before 1908] become entirely self-supporting. With the aid of Bishop Funsten, valuable property has recently been purchased for a rectory and a clergyman has been called by the vestry.

I wish to thank all the ladies of the Guild most heartily for their great kindness in placing the Guild Fund at our immediate disposal. It will make the first payment on the rectory which I trust will be made soon.

J. Roberts

Lander in 1872 were held in buildings lent by their owners for that purpose. One was on Main Street, between Second and Third Streets, belonging to Mr. James K. Moore, Sr. Another building was on the back of a lot, on Main, between First and Second Streets, owned and lent by Major Noyes Baldwin. When Bishop Spalding made his yearly visitation to Lander in 1884, he was very much encouraged to find church work established in the town. He found regular services being held and an organized church school being carried on with the wonderful help of the women of the church. The Lander Townsite Company, Eugene Amoretti, P.P. Dickinson and Frank Lowe, designed two lots for the site of the Episcopal Church on the corner of Third and Garfield. After a building committee was appointed and a subscription petition was circulated for funds, Bishops Spalding promised some financial help to apply on that fund. The cost of the project was about $2,500.00.

At first the "going was rough," to say the least. A letter written in 1885, by one of the building committee, to Mr. Roberts reads:

Dear Sir:

We had to take the pipe off the stove in the Mission room in order to put a stove in the new church. So there will be no stove in the other building. I suppose it will be too cold to hold a service with no fire, so perhaps it will be better for you to not come over next Sunday, but you can use your own will about it. We expect to have the new church ready by a week from Sunday. Have you heard anything from the pews? Major Baldwin says you told him to hold money out to pay the freight, so if you have any mercy or pity, let us have whatever money you can let us have.

The Rev. John Roberts held the first service in Trinity Church on December 27, 1885.[35] Roberts knew all the families living for miles up and down the Lander Valley well.[36] Many of the members of those families were baptized, married and buried by this missionary priest. Since no salary or fee came from serving the church in Lander, he usually decided upon the three hour ride back home to the Reservation after the evening service. If the weather were too stormy, he would sometimes sleep in the church.

Only once was Father Roberts held up and robbed on one of these night rides. A young man with a fire-arm stopped him and asked him for the money he knew had been collected at the evening service. Of course the young clergyman did not have the $1.75. He had only his father's watch, which was taken. Roberts recognized the youthful robber and said to him: "Your mother in Wales would be heartbroken to hear of this so I will not report you. Promise me not to rob and steal any more." The young man promised, but not long afterward he was arrested in another part of the territory for the same offence. He was identified by the watch.

The first notation of a service held at Milford reads, "Service at North Fork, 1885, in the schoolhouse." Regular services were held for many years at North Fork — now Milford — by Mr. Roberts for the

---

[35] *With many White settlers who were now coming into Lander Valley to make their homes, it was well past time to arrange for a resident priest at Trinity Church. Again it was "rough going." Many young men came for a short time, then went on to other and greener pastures. Perhaps this letter, addressed to a more experienced and very understanding Rev. Roberts, would explain, at least one of the reasons:*

"Reverend and Dear Brother: I was glad to hear from you as I have been obliged to run into debt on account of the expense of the horse. The keeping of the horse costs about $10.00 a month. I have received only $24.00 since last May. On $75.00 a month, I can scarcely buy provisions and coal and other necessities, much less keep a horse...Best wishes for a Happy New Year." Signed.

[36] *The windows in the nave of the church were given as memorials by Bishop Ethelbert Talbot. One window above the altar was given by Mrs. A.D. Lane in memory of her mother. The other Windows, also above the altar, were given by Trinity Sunday School children in memory of Alice Godfry, one of their number.*

benefit of the white settlers making their homes on the Popo Agie River.
"At one time," he writes, "we met regularly in the large room of the grist
mill. There, amid piles of sacks of flour and grain, we read with thankful
hearts, the Prayers, the Chants and the Psalter of our grand old service.
But the time came when the mill must be run day and night to grind the
wheat while there was a full flow of water in the river. There was nothing
to do but to adjourn to a small cabin close by, for the mill made a 'bigger
racket than the preacher.' Now we hold services in the schoolhouse. We
hope soon to have a church of our own. The past ten years, a small but
faithful band of women have been diligently working to raise funds for
that purpose. They have succeeded in realizing $500.00."

A small church, St. Paul's was completed in 1906. The men of the
congregation did the carpentry work after hauling the lumber one hundred
and fifty miles, by wagon, from Rock Springs. A good many years later
the resident priest from Lander held the Sunday service at St. Paul's in
Milford. The church stood on the little hill just south of the Popo Agie
bridge and a short distance east of the highway. The building, with its
white cross, could be seen for miles. St. Paul's has since been torn down
and even the lumber discarded.

The available record for the beginning of the church in the town of
Pavillion — a very new town in 1908 — is meager but quite satisfactory,
as far as it goes:

The Townsite company of Pavillion.
Dear Sirs:

In behalf of the Episcopal Church, I beg leave to apply
to you for a site for the church building and rectory in your
new town of Pavillion.

Signed, John Roberts

A most courteous and generous letter, in answer, was received

Rev. John Roberts:
Dear Sir:

Regarding your request for two lots for the church, I
will say we have taken up the matter with the company. We
recognize your ability as a clergyman who gets results. Believe
we could not put this matter in better hands, recommend to the
Company that the lots be given you for church purposes. We
assure you that you may expect good results. Thanking you

for the interest you have taken in the matter, we wish you an
entire success.

Signed, The Pavillion Townsite Co., Sec.

In South Pass, the Rev. John Roberts held services occasionally in a
little Episcopal church, as early as the 1890's. A church school was
organized and carried on by interested and devout Christian people, in the
absence of the priest who had many stations, miles apart, to visit.
Clergymen and ministers, passing through South Pass, would hold a
service there. Members of all recognized Christian denominations were
welcome to use the church.

This building, even at that time, was old. In 1893 it was sold for
$100.00 and torn down. Some of the lumber was used in the building of
a store which is still standing. The lots, 57 and 59, were not included in
the sale. The title was invested in the name of Bishop George Maxwell
Randall.

In Atlantic City, many years before St. Andrew's Church was built,
Father Roberts held services in the lobby of the hotel, at ranch homes and
later in the schoolhouse. In 1912,[37] $700.00 was deposited in the bank to
apply on the building fund of the new church, St. Andrew's. The Rev.
A.F. Schepp, stationed in Lander, held the first service in the new church.
Conducting services and ministering to the families of that church has
since been the great privilege and responsibility of the resident priest of
Trinity Church in Lander.

There had been no public schools on the Reservation (for settler's
children or the children of army officers to attend) until Rev. Roberts
took the case of establishing District Schools to court. Some families had
been able to keep a governess but when times were busy, she was expected
to forget lessons and help with the sewing or ironing or any other 'polite'
housework. Sometime after the turn of the century, Rev. Roberts was
successful in getting the first District School established on the Reservation.
And it was some years later before a voting precinct was allowed on the
Reservation. The nearest precinct was Milford, ten miles from the

---

[37] *The description of the lots of the site of Trinity Church in Lander, that of St.
Paul's in Milford, of St. Thomas' in Dubois, of St. Luke's in Shoshoni, of St. James' in
Riverton, of St. Matthew's in Hudson, the three church lots in Thermopolis, were all
duly recorded in Lander and the Title Deed handed to the Bishop of Wyoming who had,
at that time, the oversight of jurisdiction. (Page 31 of the* Convocation Journal *of 1912)*

Mr. Roberts, in a buffalo coat, with his horse Buckskin

Shoshone Agency. Through correspondence and many trips to the county seat at Lander, he was able to have this unjust and inconvenient condition corrected.

Rev. Roberts also saw the need of a library in Lander. Again there were many trips, by team and buckboard, to town. Every trip to meet with the committee was three hours there and three hours back. Now everyone may enjoy the privileges of a fine library.

The desperate need of a hospital in Lander was in the minds of some of its citizens long before the Bishop Randall Hospital was built. In 1904, Father Roberts wrote Bishop Funsten, suggesting to him the possibility of building a hospital. Bishop Funsten, then Bishop of Wyoming and Idaho, answered, "As to the hospital, I hardly know. Money is hard to get, but look into the cost and write me." In 1909, the Bishop wrote to Mr. Roberts again. "I mentioned the subject of the Lander hospital to your new Bishop, (Bishop Thomas). If you push the matter by offering a block, we can make a small gift of three lots toward the site of the hospital." Bishop Funsten and many others intensely interested in the project, by planning and working together, were finally successful. In his annual address to the convocation convened in Casper, June 19, 1912, Bishop Thomas said, "As this convocation convenes, the Bishop Randall Hospital at Lander will be under roof, at an approximate cost of $32,000.00 on which has already been raised $20,000.00."

The Rev. John Roberts made his trips to all outlying stations on horseback. Some stations were two or more days ride from Shoshone Agency. He had two riding ponies — one rested in the pasture while the other was on the road. "Chubby" danced on his hind legs in protest when the rider wore the necessary buffalo overcoat; the other pony, a sturdy buckskin, was a fine buffalo runner — if he could get the bit between his teeth, he was free to run as fast and as far as he wished. Buffalo hunting was formerly done by the Indians on horseback. They used their fleetest and most enduring ponies for this purpose. Riding along side of the animal in the chase, an Indian would shoot arrows or bullets into the animal until he fell. Both ponies traveled far, doing their work faithfully as long as they lived. Incidentally, both Buckskin and Chubby were known to the readers of the old *"Spirit of Missions,"* the missionary magazine of the Episcopal church.

Buckskin was still being used as a buffalo pony when Roberts bought him in 1884 from an Arapahoe on the Shoshone Indian Reservation. The

Indians brought in and sold 3,000 buffalo hide robes to the trader. From 1884 until 1909 Buckskin was used in the service of the Church. His hardiness and endurance were proverbial. He would easily go 25 to 75 miles and never seemed to be tired. Unsaddled, he would roll on the ground, then begin to graze on the prairie. The next morning he would be ready to start out. Buckskin covered the miles at a slow lope and would keep it up for hours at a time on rough prairie trails, in the deep snow and through the worst storms. He never failed to reach his destination and his equal would be hard to find. Buckskin died at the age of 32 years, a pensioner, as he deserved, on the Shoshone Mission farm. He never hurt anyone and though twice he nearly drowned his riders, a bishop and a clergyman, he brought both safely through.

The great love and respect in which Roberts held his horse, Buckskin, is reflected in a letter to John Roberts from the editor of the *Spirit of Missions:*

January 1917

The Rev. John Roberts, Wind River, Wyoming

My dear Mr. Roberts:

In going through our files we find, among other interesting photographs, one which you sent in 1912 showing "Old Buckskin" with your three children on his back. You have written on the back of the photograph: "From 1884 to 1909 he was used in the work of the Mission, and the trips he made would aggregate more than the distance around the globe." We are anxious to present this picture to the children who are readers of the Missionary Magazine of the Young Churchman...if you won't let us have a little more of a story...having this soon we would appreciate it very much. We hope to have both you and Mrs. Roberts to greet our readers at that time.

With cordial greetings from all in the office, believe me to be

Faithfully yours
Charles L. Butticher

As surely as there were many problems to be solved in the work of establishing these Mission churches, there were many delightful things that happened to Mr. Roberts.

He had gone to hold service in one of the new towns that started up just before 1906. As he walked down the one street, he felt someone touch him. He supposed it had been an attempt to rob him. Instead, he found a one hundred dollar bill in his pocket that certainly had not been there before — a wonderful amount to add to the building fund of the new church. At another time, when there seemed no available place for the service, the proprietor of a saloon kindly offered the clergyman the use of his place of business. At the service this gentleman personally passed the hat, holding it in front of each member of the congregation until he considered a fair contribution had been made. In the same tent town, Mr. Roberts could find no place to sleep until a kindly bartender offered him his bed saying, "Don't never use me no bed before daylight come." And again, he was welcomed to another new town by one of its citizens who walked up to him and said, with a big warm smile, "Well, Reverend, as soon as we heard you was in town, we closed up all the saloons." "Oh," Rev. Roberts said, "very kind of you, I'm sure, but I'm really not a drinker."

On one occasion this same missionary had ridden a long distance out in the country to officiate at a wedding. Late in the evening, when the festivities were at last over, Mr. Roberts was very thankful to share a cowboy's bed in the bunkhouse. Later still, he became conscious of someone leaning across him, speaking to his friend in a loud whisper, "Bill, Bill, want some more ice cream? She's a-meltin' fast."

Early Photo of Chief Washakie

Part 2

Chapter 1

Washakie, Chief of the Shoshones

Washakie,[38] Chief of the Shoshones, was a great man because he was a good man. By acts of war and massacre, many chiefs have been well-known for a time. Washakie's name lives on because he stood for peace and progress for his people. He wanted churches and schools for them. He realized that they would have to learn to feed themselves by farming and raising stock and later, by learning a trade or profession, since they could no longer depend on hunting.

His people, though often at peace, were many times surrounded by stronger and more numerous hostile tribes. Washakie himself was a brave fighter with great ability to command. He would have made as able an officer on the battlefield as he was an Indian Chief. He taught his followers discipline and obedience. As a young man, his prowess as a hunter and as a warrior had placed him at the head of his tribe. As Chief, he was called upon to repel the attack of their enemies on every side — Sioux, Cheyenne, Arapahoe, Blackfeet, Crows and others. In fighting the latter, he received an arrow wound in the cheek which left a scar. He was known among Indians, far and wide, as the Shoshone Chief with the scarred cheek. But he was noted also for his loyalty to the government and for his friendship for the Whites. Washakie rendered valuable service to the military in subduing hostile tribes. Consequently he had only to apply for arms and ammunition at any army post in the west and his wants were supplied. On one occasion, fifty rifles, with ammunition, were given him to be distributed among his warriors.

Washakie was born in the Flathead country, Montana, in 1798. His father was a Flathead, his mother, a Shoshone. When a young man,

---

[38] *In a letter to one of his friends, a Mr. Parks, Roberts reported that the officers named the military post on the Reservation, Fort Washakie, in honor of the good old Chief of the Shoshones. "This good old man told me himself that his name was Wus-suk-ke, which is the name of the rawhide rattle that some of the Shoshones use in some of their dances. But he said, My army friends could not pronounce my name properly so they called me, 'Washakie.' By this name he will be known in history."*

Chief Washakie with his council, circa 1883. Identification of group members:

1. George Wesaw
2. George Washakie
3. Aohagahamma

4. Tigee
5. Tibsin Tigee
6. Dish Washakie

7. Unidentified
8. Chief Washakie
9. Biagoosa

10. Matavish
11. Thought to be Jim Washakie
12. Bonzi

13. Panzook
14. Zagiva or Zagavatsie

Washakie left the Flatheads and joined his mother's people. Little is known of his early career. When questioned about the exploits of his youth, his answer was, "As a young man I delighted in war. When my tribe was at peace, I wandered off alone in search of an enemy." Later in life he conquered a Crow Chief in single combat, on the Big Wind River,[39] then let him return to his own people.

Washakie's second wife was captured in a battle with the Crows. She was a young girl when taken. Washakie raised her and when she was grown, he married her. Charles Washakie, his son, painted a picture on elk hide of this battle, at the direction of his father.

Chief Washakie was a man of commanding and distinguished appearance, tall and well built. He moved with great natural dignity. He wore his hair long, hanging below his shoulders. In his later years, he wore a cotton shirt, a scarf or handkerchief around his neck, held in place by having the ends pulled through openings in a large round shell. Around his hips was wrapped a blanket which hung to the ankles. High leggings and beaded moccasins completed the costume. When Washakie was young he wore his war bonnet on special occasions. This war bonnet usually hung to the floor and what a picture he made with his six feet in height and his dignity in bearing. The intelligence and benevolence shown in his face would point him out as the great chief which he was.

Washakie was presented with a very fine saddle by President Grant. It was sent to him through Dr. Irwin, the Indian agent at Shoshone Agency. The old chief received it without a word. Dr. Irwin pressed him several

---

[39] *"I have tried," Roberts wrote in his journal, "to gather some data concerning the battle on Crowheart Butte but what I gathered was very scant. The Shoshones are very reticent about their past history. Like other Snake Indians they are extremely secretive in character. They tell me that under Washakie's leadership, they had a great battle with the Crows in the vicinity of Crowheart Butte, but the old men say that they do not remember besieging the enemy there or placing the heart of the Crow Chief on a pole on the top - according to the tradition come down to us through White trappers of that time.*

"The Shoshone name for this noted land mark is 'Hi-am-be,' crow or raven, its heart. Why it is so called they don't appear to know any more than why the Coeur d ' Alene in Idaho is so called heart of an owl. I have seen a photo of the hill. If I can secure a copy I shall have great pleasure in mailing it to you, also one of the To-go-te or Two-go-te. He was a Sheepeater or Mountain Shoshone. He, with one or two others of his clan, were more familiar with the mountain passes than other Shoshones and was designated by Washakie to guide President Arthur and his party from Fort Washakie to the Yellowstone Park in 1883. Since that time, the trail they took over the Divide has been called To-go-te Pass."

times for some expression of sentiment, saying that the President would be waiting for some word. Finally, the chief walked to the window of the office. While looking out toward the peaks of the great Rockies, and with his back to those whom he was addressing, he said, "Say to President Grant that when a favor is done for a Frenchman, the Frenchman feels it in his head and his tongue speaks; when a kindness is done for an Indian, the Indian feels it in his heart and the heart has no tongue."

Washakie was not adverse to fighting but when his men wanted to attack the United States soldiers at Fort Bridger in 1863, he advised strongly against it. He told them they were going against the men who made the guns. "You will go into battle like brave warriors but you will come out like whipped dogs." This time the warriors disregarded his warning and made their attack on the soldiers, under General Conner, from a canyon. The Indians fired the first volley and thirty saddles of the soldiers' were emptied. Then the soldiers brought up a mountain howitzer and began firing at the Indians. There was little avenue of escape for them. Many were slaughtered. A few escaped by running through the ranks of the soldiers and swimming the river with the temperature at forty degrees below zero. They were shot at in the stream and nearly all killed. The Indians were in possession of a few rifles which they had obtained through some French Canadian traders and the Hudson Bay Trading Company.

Dr. James Irwin
Reservation Agent 1882 - 1884

Washakie's band of Shoshones had camped and hunted in Utah, Idaho and Wyoming. Many rivers, mountains and valleys in this part of the country bear witness to this by having Shoshone names. They were familiar with the topography of these places. When the government required the Shoshones to settle on a Reservation, Washakie was allowed to choose the place to be reserved for his people. When the officials met with him at Fort Bridger in 1868, he was asked to make his selection by longitude and latitude but the old chief declined. With a twinkle in his eye, he said "Bye and bye I hope we may all meet there but for the present, the mountains and rivers will be the boundaries." This region was known to the Shoshones as "Eu-ar-eye" which means "warm valley." When emigrants passed in great numbers through the Shoshone country of Wyoming in 1850, Washakie and his people exercised great forbearance, following the instructions of the government agents. They aided overland travelers in recovering strayed or lost stock, helped the emigrants to cross dangerous fords and to find water and grass at the end of the day. So friendly and helpful were Washakie and the members of his band that nine thousand emigrants signed a paper commending their treatment.

It is the general opinion that the Shoshones drove other nations of Indians from what is now their Reservation. Perhaps more than a hundred and fifty years ago, the Sioux, Cheyenne, Crow and Arapahoe were driven north by them. There are mountains and rivers with other than Shoshone names which point to the fact.

Every commissioner that visited the Shoshones was cordially received by Washakie and no treaty ever failed to be ratified when it was Washakie's decision. Opposed as he was to the allotting of his land in severalty to the Indians, the allotting agent had but to show his commission and Washakie at once assented.

Washakie was for many years in the employ of the American and Hudson Bay Fur Company and was long the valued companion of army officers, White hunters and trappers. When Fort Brown was established on the site of Lander, Wyoming, in 1869, Washakie met the soldiers and avowed his friendship for them. He frequently served as scout against Cheyenne, Sioux, Arapahoe, Ute and other tribes.

Washakie was married four times. There were ten children and many grandchildren. He always spoke the name of God, Our Father, as he called Him, with the greatest reverence, bowing his head. For many years he was well disposed to the "White robes," as he referred to the Episcopal Church. He was baptized by the Rev. John Roberts on January 25, 1897. For seventeen years Washakie and Rev. John Roberts were personal friends, living as neighbors and working in the interest of the Indians.

Many long hours they spent together in consultation regarding the things intended for the uplift of the Redmen and in friendly visits. To be the friend of Washakie was to be bound by a tie that could not be broken. Washakie gave one hundred and sixty acres of land to Roberts for the site of the Episcopal chapel, permanent Mission school and farm. This gift was ratified by a special Act of Congress.

Washakie said, "Let us do all we can for the young people growing up around us. One thing I tell them and tell them, the Whites are your true friends. Be true to them. One thing more I want to see and my heart will be at peace. I want to see the church and the school built for my people, by the 'white robes.' To you my friend, John Roberts, I give the land. I cannot now live long. All my old warriors are gone. I alone, am left. My hair is white. I do not know which one of my sons will be Chief after me. My heart goes out to you. I shake hands with you."

At the time of his death Washakie was a devout member of the Episcopal Church. A young, somewhat self assertive, young minister went up to Washakie and said, "Washakie, I want to teach you about God." The grand old Chief replied, "Young man, do you know our dear Father yourself?" and he bowed his head.

The story of how Washakie's thirst led to the discovery of the Pilot Butte oil field was told to Rev. Roberts by the Chief. Washakie told him that he and a party of Shoshone friends were on a buffalo hunt and had made a kill near where the Pilot oil field was later located. "I was skinning a big bull and I became thirsty. My son was in the party so I gave him a tin cup and told him to go beyond the trees and see if there was not a spring of water. He soon returned and said it was not water but grease. We looked at it afterward and found the oil spring. We used it for many years for medicinal purposes."

When Washakie signed the treaty between the United States government and the Shoshones, ceding the land containing the Thermopolis Hot Springs to the government, he expressed the wish that the Springs should be held free of access to all people, rich and poor, forever.

"Even in the early years of his chieftainship, Washakie was the great power behind the Shoshone Tribe. He ruled with regal authority and what he said was respected by the Indians and Whites alike. His great influence preserved his tribe not only as a friend but as an ally of the White people in their struggle here. It was his pride that he had never allowed a white man's blood to be shed when he could prevent it." This tribute was paid to Washakie by an army officer. Also, the Rev. John Roberts was loud in his praise of his abilities. He said that Chief Washakie of the Shoshones and Black Coal of the Arapahoes, were among our greatest men.

Chief Washakie suffered a great grief in the death of his eldest son, Nan-nang-gai, Snow bird, in 1861 or 1862. A band of Shoshones, under the leadership of Washakie, went on a buffalo hunt to the Big Horn Basin. On their return home to Utah, they camped by night on the Sweetwater, Wyoming, at the crossing of the old government road. The next morning they were attacked by a war party of two hundred Sioux who had come across their trail and had followed it with the purpose of attacking their camp. As soon as the Shoshones recovered from their surprise, about one hundred of their warriors charged the enemy, who fell back to a quaking ash grove that was nearby. The Sioux then rushed forward and cut off many of the Shoshones' horses and started to drive them away. There was great excitement in the camp where preparations were instantly made to follow the marauders.

In the first charge, Washakie killed a Sioux. While standing with a group of Shoshones over his fallen foe, his eldest son rode up, late for the battle. Washakie reproved Nan-nang-gai for his tardiness saying, "Where have you been so long? I am an old man, have killed the Sioux while you have come up after the fight." Snow bird felt the rebuke keenly and, turning his horse toward the enemy, he said, "I will make for myself a great name or die in the attempt." He rode toward the enemy alone. When within a few yards of the Sioux, he fell, pierced by a number of arrows and bullets. He had no sooner fallen when his body was literally cut to pieces in sight of his father. Washakie's war whoop was then changed to a wail. The older chief, backed by his warriors, fought desperately to avenge his son, crying and wailing as he fought. At sunset the Sioux retreated, leaving several of their number dead on the field and bearing with them many severely wounded.

The battle was over. Washakie's heart was filled with grief and remorse. Nan-nang-gai, Snow Bird, was gone. He never ceased to mourn the loss of this, his eldest son. He always felt that his hasty words brought about the death of the young man. This story was told to the Rev. John Roberts by Chief Washakie himself.

Washakie's sense of justice was very keen even when it pertained to his own family. His son, Jim, was drinking in a place where a woman was selling bootleg whiskey. Her son, hearing her screams when Jim became abusive, rushed in and fatally shot the young Indian man.

The funeral procession gathering in front of Chief Washakie's cabin where he died, February 20, 1900.

There was a false rumor that Washakie threatened to avenge his son by killing the first White man he met. How different was the true story! The Rev. John Roberts went at once to the Chief's home to express his sympathy and to offer any possible help. In speaking with the clergyman, Washakie said, "The White man did not kill my son. Whiskey killed him."

Washakie's age was established by his relatives, particularly by his nephew, John Enos, the son of his sister. The Flatheads kept account of their ages, the Shoshones did not. Enos declared that Washakie was eleven years older than he, that Washakie was born in 1798 which made him 102 years of age when he died in 1900. It is certain that Washakie had been one of the chiefs of the Shoshones for many years and Head Chief for half a century. He died on February 20, 1900, in the little cabin he had built for himself.

· Washakie was buried with full military honors in the post cemetery at Fort Washakie, February 22, at 2:00 p.m. The great Chief's funeral was very impressive, with at least 1500 people present, representing many walks of life. The post commander, Lieutenant Overton, was in attendance with the full troop of cavalry from Fort Washakie. At 1:30 p.m. The troops formed and presented swords as the body was borne from the home in the casket. Washakie's horse, draped in deep mourning, was led by a trooper of the garrison immediately behind a caisson drawn by four black mules furnished by the commander. Next in order came the pallbearers:

Shoshone	Honorary
White St. Clair	James Moore
Tigee	F. G. Burnett
Timoke	Mr. Clark
Havee	E. F. Cheney
Andrew Bazil	B.F. Lowe
Moon-havie	Wm. McCabe

The Episcopal funeral service was conducted by the Rev. John Roberts and the Rev. Sherman Coolidge. In addition to the regular service, a prayer in the Shoshone language was read by Rev. Roberts. Three volleys were fired over the open grave by the troops, then taps was sounded by the bugler. Thus passed from mortal eye all that remained of the famous warrior, Washakie, Chief of the Shoshones. He had always been an ally of the Whites, acting as scout and guide for General Crook, a warm

Reverends Roberts and Coolidge leading the cortège for Chief Washakie's burial in the post cemetery at Ft. Washakie.

friend of Grant, Sherman and other leading officers of the United States Army. Too much cannot be said of the noblest Chief and warrior that the Whites ever knew.

The following tribute to the memory of Chief Washakie was issued by the commanding officer at the fort:

General Order No. 2, Fort Washakie, Wyoming, February 21, 1900.

With sorrow is announced the death of Washakie. For 50 years, as chief of the Shoshones, he has held the love and confidence of his tribe. His friendship for the Whites began with their earliest settlement in this section. His great influence preserved his tribe as not only a friend but an ally of our people in their struggle here. It was his pride that he had never allowed a White man's blood to be shed when he could prevent it.

Washakie was of a commanding presence and his resemblance in face to Washington was often remarked. His countenance was one of rugged strength mingled with kindness. His military service is an unbroken record for gallantry. Officers now wearing a star fought with him in their subaltern days. The respect and friendship of these former commanders was prized to the day of his death. Washakie was a great man, for he was a good man and a brave one. The spirit of his loyalty and courage will speak to soldiers; the memory of his love for his own people will linger to assist them in their troubles and he will never be forgotten as long as the mountain and streams of Wyoming, which was his home, bear his name.

His last request was a Christian burial in the Post Cemetery with the soldiers who were his friends.

The post commander directs that Washakie be buried with military honors, in the post cemetery at 2:00 p.m. tomorrow and that a copy of this order, announcing his death, be mailed to officers under whom he served the government.

By order of Clough Overton, 1st Lieutenant,
1st Cavalry, Command Post.
Aubrey Lippincott, 2nd Lieutenant,
1st Cavalry, Adjutant.

The Rev. John Roberts, in his official announcement of Washakie's death, wrote, "I am grieved to report the death of an Indian churchman,

Washakie. With Washakie, the chieftainship of the Shoshones passed away. No successor will be appointed to his office. The present policy of the government in dealing with Indians, is to break up the tribal relations and to deal with them as individuals and to prepare them for citizenship."

In 1905, the War Department erected a granite monument over Washakie's grave on the east side of which were chiseled, in deep letters, the words, "Washakie 1804-1900; [the date of his birth should be 1798.) On the north side is cut, "A wise ruler;" on the west, "Chief of the Shoshones;" and on the south side is inscribed, "Always loyal to the government and to his White brothers."

Old Chief Washakie very gladly availed himself of the help that a Reservation and the presence of a United States garrison afforded him in keeping his people under control. Loyal as they were to him, some turbulent spirits among them would break out in mischief. State stations and emigrant trains would be robbed. But swift and sure punishment was invariably meted out to the guilty ones upon their return. Before the second tribe was placed on this Reservation, these prairies proved a veritable "Land of Eden" to many settlers.

My grandfather was well acquainted with the people that came to Central Wyoming in the 1880's. Among them were the three old pioneers, William McCabe, John Sheard and Thomas Cook. My grandfather wrote a brief account of their lives which he left with his other personal letters. He must have felt that it would help us to see the way people lived in the early settling of our state:

"William McCabe, John Sheard, and Thomas Cook were," according to Roberts, "long time friends, grim old pioneers of this region. McCabe was a U.S. Indian scout and a veteran of many Indian wars. The three were freighters of early days, allies of friendly Indians, the terror of hostile bands. Two of them were staunch churchmen. McCabe, not long ago, handed me $5.00 for Missions in memory of the *auld man* — Arch bishop Whately, Dublin, Ireland." An unidentified newspaper clipping in the Roberts collections tells us that, "Shortly after the abandonment of Fort Washakie, old friend William McCabe, left here for Sheridan, Wyoming. He will be stationed at Fort McKenzie which is but two miles from the northern metropolis of the state.'" Mr. McCabe has been connected with Fort Washakie as a government scout for more than a quarter of a century and he knew, in detail, nearly every movement made by the troops of the post from its infancy to its final abandonment. He can relate many interesting narratives of frontier days and our people surely regret that it became necessary for him to leave our midst."

"At the time of his death," Roberts wrote, "he was the oldest living Indian scout, having come into the Lander area at the time of the formation of the Wind River Indian Reservation, which was then much larger than at present. After coming here in the early 60's, he served as scout for many Indian expeditions of the army. He was a veteran of the Mexican war and chief of the scouts in the Bates battle where he gave valuable and fearless service in 1874. One of his important duties, while working for the government, was that of being a wagon boss over the Indian freighters when they hauled goods overland from Rawlins to Shoshone Agency."

In the photo the man with the watch chain is Thomas Cook, "one of the worthy pioneers of Lander, a shoemaker by trade, also an expert farmer and stockman." The one on the left is John Sheard, whom Roberts described as "one of the indomitable string-team wagon freighters, who freighted between Rawlins and Fort Washakie. With his string team of sixteen to eighteen horses, he hauled eight or nine thousand pounds over all but impassable wagon trails, steep and dangerous, through winter snows and spring mud. Much could be written of his thrilling and humorous experiences. He kept to the road till over eighty. He was well educated and claimed to have been formally associated with Bill Nye in establishing his famous paper in Laramie. He died at an advanced age at the poor farm at Baggs or Dixon, Wyoming. Once I remember driving past his camp on the road on the Beaver Divide in a terrible snow storm. His horses were tied to the wagon wheels, all knotted up with cold. In his tent close by, a sage brush fire was roaring through the stove pipe.

"Some days after returning home, I found him seated by the warm kitchen range at the Mission, at the end of his journey. He had one of my little daughters on his knee, singing for her at the top of his voice, Mrs. Herman's *Better Land*. I asked him how he got along in the storm on the Divide. He said, 'Well, sire, it blew one continuous blast for three days and nights, but we had plenty of hay and grain for the horses and a tent as good as a house.' Then he dropped his chin on his chest and muttered to himself, 'the hay and grain played out on us the second day,' but looking up, he said quickly, 'We made it.' On being asked on another occasion how he managed when the wagon brakes broke on a steep mountain side, the old man replied, 'We came down as fast as the laws of gravity would permit.'"

Another time on delivering damaged freight, he shook his finger at me saying, "don't you say a word, if you knew what I came through this trip!" On asking him how he got through, he replied, "We hooked on two strings to a wagon (30 or 40 horses) and floated her through."

Left to right: John Sheard, Freighter/Teamster;
Thomas Cook with watch chain, Lander Pioneer & Businessman; William McCabe, Indian Scout

Three generations of Shoshone women by Andrew Roedel. He sent this photo to Mr. Roberts in 1945 for possible identification of the old woman as Sacajawea. Rev. Roberts was blind by that time, and could not offer an opinion. The middle age woman standing is believed to be Barbara Myers, Sacajawea's granddaughter.

Chapter 2

Sacajawea

The day after Mr. Roberts' arrival at the Agency, the Indian agent, Dr. James Irwin, took him to see a very, very old Shoshone woman who lived in a small cabin at the agency. As a missionary clergyman, Mr. Roberts came to know this old lady very well, though he was more interested in her as an aged person who needed care and attention than he was in the fact that she was Sacajawea, the Shoshone girl guide of the Lewis and Clark Expedition.

The following account was written by the Rev. John Roberts, regarding his acquaintance with, and his knowledge of, Sacajawea:

> The day after my arrival on the Shoshone and Bannock Indian Reservation, February 10, 1883, I went to the office of the United States Indian Agent, Dr. Irwin, where a few Indians were assembled. Most of the tribes were absent on their annual winter buffalo hunt. Among those present was Bazil, one of the head men of the tribe. He was probably nearing eighty years of age and a very fine representative of an Indian. I was introduced to Bazil by Dr. Irwin. Bazil spoke very little English though I was told he could speak French.
>
> Dr. Irwin, the Indian agent, took me to Bazil's camp which was about one hundred yards from the agent's office, to see an aged woman who was called "Bazil's Mother". She was seated on the ground in a teepee. Her hair was white and she had the appearance of being very, very old. Bazil said she was his mother and that she was about one hundred years old. Bazil, whom I came to know very well, was really her nephew and her adopted son. Bazil proved to be a very dutiful son to her. He cared for her faithfully and had his daughters and other women of the tribe see to her every need. The Indian agent had her supplied with beef, flour, coffee and other groceries, even a little tobacco which she enjoyed smoking.
>
> Dr. Irwin told me that one time his friend, Bazil, came to him and demanded permission to pitch his mother's teepee close to his, Dr. Irwin's house. "For," said he, "I am going on

a buffalo hunt and I want you to take special care of my mother. She has been a great friend to the White people in early days."

Dr. Irwin alluded to her connection with the Lewis and Clark Expedition many times. He was keenly interested in the subject. Sacajawea had told the story of her journey to the Pacific to her good friend, Mrs. Irwin. The record of this story, carefully written by Mrs. Irwin, was later burned with other valuable papers and agency records. Sacajawea never boasted of her journey and great service to the White people. At various times she spoke about her adventure to pioneers living on the Reservation and to the Army officers. On the other hand, and until the last years of her life, she kept it a secret, for if the fact should be published about her leading the expedition of White explorers across the Indian hunting country, it would have brought only reproach and scorn from the members of her tribe. Bazil would not have mentioned the fact to Dr. Irwin if he had not been anxious for the welfare of his mother during his absence.

Although Sacajawea had been silent concerning the journey, during her later years she used to entertain members of her immediate family by relating to them some of her experiences while on that journey. She told them she had seen the great waters toward the setting sun; that she had seen a fish as big as a house. Captain Clark also refers, in his diary, to a dead whale which had been found washed ashore. She told of having to jump in the river to save the valuable papers which had been thrown into the water when the boat tipped over.

After the death of Charboneau, her husband, who was part French and part Indian, Sacajawea went to visit kindred tribes of her people. For some years the Shoshones and the Whites lost sight of her. She spent several years with Comanches who are related to the Shoshones and who speak the same language. But the homing instinct led her, at the latter part of her life, to seek her own people in Wyoming.[40]

---

[40] *The story of Sacajawea has been a long and controversial one. When my grandfather first came to the Reservation, he had little knowledge of the Lewis and*

Clark expedition. At that time the news of their great trip and its significance was not really known all over the country nor abroad. Many people coming to the Reservation in the later years often wished to state their views on this Indian woman and tell us the many reasons that the woman who my Grandfather knew as "Sacajawea," could not have been the guide of the Lewis and Clark Expedition. These people did not know her or meet her personally, nor did they know how to speak the Shoshone language, making it impossible for them to communicate with the elder people of the tribe.

Though I, too, have no first hand knowledge of Sacajawea or her descendants, the following accounts were carefully recorded by my grandfather, John Roberts, who knew her personally.

When I was young I often asked my grandfather why he didn't just tell them that the young Shoshone girl was the guide of the Lewis and Clark Expedition. He answered, "If they don't believe the facts as they have been stated, there is no reason to trouble them with more argument. Let the old Indian lady sleep in peace. She has earned her rest." My grandfather was completely unconcerned when people disputed his word about her identity. He knew that she was the guide of the Expedition and was satisfied that he was sure of the facts.

The people that knew, saw and added their testimony about the identity of this Shoshone woman, were not of this century. The term "Tourism" had not been coined. They didn't care or even dream that thousands of people would cross the Reservation and turn toward the Shoshone Cemetery just to see a grave on the hillside. In the later years of my grandfather's life, he had many people within the United States, and some from other countries, stop and ask him for a complete history of the Indians, but even at that time very few of them expressed an interest in the cemetery.

There was no reason, no purpose for the old military men at the Fort, the government employees, the early settlers, the old Indians or my grandfather to make up the story of Sacajawea, or to identify her as the guide for the Lewis and Clark Expedition. What would be their reason? Her family, and the old Indians that identified her as the guide and told her story, would probably have remained silent if they had realized it would have caused so much interest among the Whites.

No one in Rev. Roberts' time was looking to exploit Sacajawea or her final resting place as a tourist attraction. Another consideration concerning her relative anonymity is suggested in the following letter to the Sioux City Journal from Harry Simonds:

February 14, 1923

The Editor, The Sioux city Journal, Sioux City, Iowa:

   It is really a fact that Sacajawea was deserted by her renegade husband. She lived on the Wind River Reservation all the rest of her days and died there at the home of her son, Baptiste, the child she bore to Charboneau and which child she carried on her trip with the explorers. There is no circumstantial evidence about it. It is a known positive fact that she did live and she was known there to the Agency Superintendents from the late 70's on. There is nothing strange that she was not heard of often. She was proud of her achievement but the Shoshones looked upon her about as we look upon Benedict Arnold, for it was she that aided the hated Whites to explore and fasten themselves more firmly to the Indian country. Her son, Baptiste, also lived and died on the Wind River Reservation and is buried near his mother in the Shoshone Cemetery.

James I. Patten, who was appointed United States Indian Agent of the Shoshones in the seventies and who spoke their language, was convinced that the claim of the old Shoshone woman, Bazil's mother, was genuine. Mr. F.G. Burnett, the U.S. government farmer and a resident on the Reservation for many years, was well acquainted with Sacajawea and her two sons. He spoke with her many times about her journey to the Pacific. Mr. Richard Morse, a government employee at Shoshone Agency for many years, also knew Sacajawea personally. Many fine pioneer men and women of the seventies and eighties, believed the story of Bazil's mother.

James Patten, Reservation Agent,
1878-1879
(U.S. Indian Agent to the Shoshones)

Baptiste, Sacajawea's son,[41] I knew over a period of years, up to his death. He had a large family whose descendants

---

[41] *May 27, 1922*
Dear Mr. Haas:

Concerning Baptiste, the brother of the adopted Bazil, I really do not know much. I remember him well, but he was in no way a prominent Indian like good old Bazil who was a loyal and true friend to the government at all times.

(signed) J. Roberts

Roberts notes state that: Bazil's name as a child was Pomp. Wit-o-gan, son of Baptiste, told J. Roberts that his grandmother guided the first Whites across the country to the great sea toward the setting sun and that she carried his father, Baptiste, then a baby, all the way on her back.

The Director of the Bureau of American Ethnology, Smithsonian Institution, Washington, D.C., confirms these facts and the commissioner of Indian Affairs writes:

"In answer to your letter of Dec...you are advised the 'Bird Woman' or 'Sacajawea' died at her son's home [on] the Wind River Reservation near Fort Washakie in Wyoming on April 9, 1884, and was buried at that place." Who should know better about this matter than the office that deals directly with the Indians and in which office the tribal census rolls (See Appendix #1, under "Lodge #118") are kept? This office also says 'She remained among the Shoshones in Wyoming and when the Wind River Reservation was created, took up her abode there with her son, and there she died, near Fort Washakie, April 9, 1884, about one hundred years of age.' Anyone caring to investigate the details

of the facts of the matter had better to go to Fort Washakie, Wyoming and there, talk with living witnesses who knew her well. Look up the records at the Agency and become convinced that the facts are so well established that there is no doubt whatsoever that Sacajawea is buried therein as stated.

(s) Harry L. Simonds

---

are now living on the Reservation. He spent his time hunting and fishing to supply the needs of his family. His son, Wyt-to-gan, told me one time that his father had been carried, when a baby, on his mother's back, across the mountains when she led the White men toward the setting sun to the great Pacific.

When Baptiste died in 1885 he was buried, according to the ancient custom of the Shoshones, in a canyon west of the agency and there let down between two crags forty feet deep. Years later, a search for the body, showed a mountain slide had forever buried the bones. This was at the head of Dry Creek.

Bazil, the nephew and adopted son of Sacajawea, in whose camp she spent her last years, died a few years after his mother, in 1886. He was buried about four miles from the agency. Subsequently, his body was buried beside the grave of Sacajawea, in the Shoshone Indian cemetery. Bazil, himself, was a noted pioneer and guide. It was he who guided Major Baldwin who was then in command of Fort Bridger, when the Major made a trip of exploration to the Lander Valley.

To go back two or three years before the sons died: "A messenger came to me on the morning of April 9, 1884, to say that Bazil's mother had died during the night on her shakedown of quilts, blankets and pelts, in the log cabin where she lived. The agent had a coffin made for her and sent some of the employees to dig her grave. She was buried on the eastern slope of a hill a mile west of the agency where there were already two graves of White people who had been killed by hostile, raiding Indians. Sacajawea was the first Indian in this burial ground which, subsequently, had been set apart by the Indian Office as a Shoshone cemetery. The burial of Sacajawea took place late in the afternoon of the day on which she died. Those in attendance were her immediate family, the Indian agent and some of the employees. I read, over her grave, the Burial Service of the Episcopal Church."

A concrete column about two feet square and three feet high marks the grave of Sacajawea. It was placed there by H. E. Wadsworth,[42] a one time Indian agent in charge of the Reservation. On the face of the column is embedded a bronze tablet given by Judge Timothy Burke of Cheyenne, Wyoming. The inscription on the tablet was prepared by Dr. Grace Raymond Hebard and it reads,

Sacajawea
Died April 9th, 1884
A guide with Lewis and Clark Expedition
Identified by Rev. John Roberts
Who officiated at her burial

By the side of the Sacajawea grave is that of Bazil. Dr. Grace Hebard, the Wyoming historian, had a massive granite stone placed near these graves in memory of Baptiste, Sacajawea's son.

---

[42] *December 29, 1941*
Dear Dr. Roberts:

I came to the Lander Valley in the spring of 1885 and being at that time barely 20 years of age, everything pertaining to the Indian was especially interesting to me. I often visited Shoshone Agency and Fort Washakie and delighted in talking to the older members of both tribes. Among them was the outstanding character of Chief Washakie with whom I became more or less acquainted.

In one of our talks of the old days among the Shoshones, he mentioned Sacajawea, calling her "that old woman, Bazil's mother." As time went on I became more and more interested in that famous character and missed no opportunity of learning more of her and her life after she returned to her people there at Shoshone Agency...You, having officiated at the burial of this woman, it occurred to me as being the one of all persons who could identify her grave.

On My request, you accompanied me to the Indian cemetery and pointed out the exact grave in question. The grave was then temporarily marked. Shortly after this I happened to mention your identification of Sacajawea's grave to Hon. Timothy Burke, then U.S. Attorney for the District of Wyoming. He immediately became interested and requested the privilege of supplying a bronze tablet to be affixed to the marker I should erect. I was more than glad to accept this offer as no government funds were available for such a purpose. I called in the Agency carpenter, Gabriel Jorgenson, and the Agency blacksmith, William L. Smith, and we together visited the grave and planned the shaft which was made by these two worthy employees. The tablet arrived in due time and was duly affixed to the shaft. I am not certain as to the exact date of the placing of the shaft and the tablet, probably in 1904 or 1905, but you probably know the exact date.

I made proper report of the placing of the marker to the Indian office in Washington and suggested that this marker was to serve until a more substantial and suitable one could be provided by the government. That this has never been done is a disgrace to the Indian Service and to the government. I hope that this little account will be of value to you in answering questions regarding the matter.

H.E. Wadsworth, Special Agent
U.S. Indian Service, Retired

Since August 25, 1963, a new monument has been dedicated to the memory of Sacajawea. It was erected at her grave in the Shoshone Indian cemetery by the Wyoming organization of the Daughters of the American Revolution. The six foot monument was carved from Wind River granite. It replaces the old, smaller one.

On November 25, 1905, Roberts wrote the following to the Wyoming historian, Grace Raymond Hebard:

My dear Madam:

I don't think that any photograph of Sacajawea was ever taken, but the old people tell me that one of her granddaughters (who is now herself a grandmother) looks very much like her when she was comparatively young. Both her sons, Baptiste, whom the heroine carried on her back during the Expedition, and Pomp or Bazil, died soon after their mother of old age. The old lady was 100 years old when she died. Her grave is here nearby the Mission, in the Indian cemetery on the hill. It is U.S. ground.

Though Sacajawea was known on the Reservation in her later years as "Bazil's Mother," Mr. Lewis Zimms, who sculpted a statue of Sacajawea after careful research in the Smithsonian Institution, spelled her name 'Sacajawea,' undoubtedly the way Captain Clark gave it. The Shoshones here called her, "Wad-ze-wipe," (Lost Woman) or "Bah-ribo," (Water White Man) and "Boo-e-nive," (Grass Maiden). But surely the name by which she will be known in history will be that given her in the Lewis and Clark Journals, Sacajawea, which means Boat Launcher.

In 1924, Dr. Charles Eastman, Sioux Indian Physician and well known author and lecturer, was especially commissioned by the Indian Department Office to investigate Sacajawea's identity. In the fall of 1924, Andrew Bazil, the grandson of Sacajawea, offered to locate the site of his father's grave made nearly 40 years before. Bazil was wrapped in a sheet and blanket and the body taken by a few Indians up Mill Creek, then placed in a gulch which caved down and covered the body. (Reported to be the first canyon left of Crooked Creek Canyon.) A wallet containing valuable documents was buried with him; papers which had belonged to Sacajawea.

The wallet was found lying beneath Bazil's skull. The contents had been so ruined by moisture and the passage of time that nothing could be deciphered. An old saddle lay across the feet, and beside the skeleton was a handsome pipe of peace. On January 12, 1925 the bones were reinterred beside those of Sacajawea.

Dr. Eastman submitted testimonies of three Indian nations — the Shoshones in Wyoming, Comanches in Oklahoma, and Gros Ventres in North Dakota and finally reported that after 60 years of wandering from her own tribe, she returned to her own people at Fort Washakie and lived the remainder of her life with her sons, until she died April 9, 1884.

There is abundant evidence in Fort Bridger that Baptiste and Bazil both were there because on Mr. Carter's account books we find the name of Baptiste bringing in furs and taking away merchandise in payment.

Dr. Hebard had a granite head stone placed in memory of Baptiste near his mother's grave which reads:

> Dedicated to the memory of Baptiste Charboneau,
> Papoose of the Lewis and Clark Expedition 1805-1806.
> Son of Sacajawea - Born Feb. 11, 1805.
> Died on this Reservation 1885.
> Buried West in the Wind River Mountains...A.D. 1933

In another old letter, Rev. Roberts writes: "I knew Sacajawea well. There is no doubt in my mind that she is the Shoshone woman who guided the Lewis and Clark Expedition. Charboneau's wife was said to have died at Mandan but he lived with the Indians and probably had more than one wife. I, as well as other White men on the Reservation, was reluctant to believe her story until she told of many aspects of that trip that would not have been known to anyone who had not participated in it."

On my Parish Register of Burials, I recorded her burial under the date of April 9, 1884, as Bazil's Mother, Shoshone, age one hundred years. Date of death, April 9, resident of Shoshone Agency. Cause of death, old age. Place of burial, Shoshone Burial Grounds, Shoshone Agency.

Signature of Clergyman,
John Roberts

The Markley/Crofts archives contain further testimony to the identity of Sacajawea. Files are available at Coe Library, University of Wyoming.

~~~

Annually, on Memorial Day, five to six hundred Shoshones assemble in the cemetery to decorate the graves there, with a profusion of wild and artificial flowers. A detail from the American Legion Post in Lander (the county seat) comes over to do honor, to the memory of their Indian comrades-in-arms, resting there. And they invariably dip the flag at the grave of Sacajawea in honor of her heroic service to the country. Sacajawea's grave overlooks the beautiful Little Wind River Valley. Standing there, one sees close by, the Shoshone Indian Mission School. At a distance of about two miles are the buildings of Fort Washakie, garrisoned by U.S. troops, in pioneer days. We see also at about the same distance, the buildings of the former Shoshone Agency. Two miles further down the valley are the buildings of the Government School, which has done a fine work for fifty-one years in preparing the Shoshones and Arapahoes for American citizenship. We see also the glistening waters of the Little Wind River and of Trout Creek hurrying down the valley from this elevation of one mile above sea level toward their destination in the Gulf of Mexico. We see, at the bottom of the valley, six miles away, great clouds of steam rising up from the famous Washakie Hot Springs. To the north, at a distance of seventy miles, arise the Washakie Needles, named in honor of the great Chief of the Shoshones. To the south is the Beaver Range of mountains. Far off to the east are the Owl Creek and the Rattlesnake mountains; to the west, close by us are the towering mountains of the main range of the Rockies, through the grim passes of which Sacajawea led the Expedition of 1805 and 1806, when no other guide was available to find the Indian trails. (See photo page 41)

Chapter 3

Sherman Coolidge
He-des-tche-wa, the Young Arapahoe

The Rev. Sherman Coolidge was born in the year 1860, a full blooded Arapahoe Indian (a fact of which he was always proud) and a member of that tribe which had lived from time immemorial on the western plains. A fierce and warlike people, they were intellectually the equal of the White race.

This little boy was given the name of He-des-tche-wa, (Runs on Top) by his parents. His father, Van-nas-du-hut, (Big Heart) was one of the tribal chiefs.

According to Arapahoe custom, He-des-tche-wa must have spent a great deal of his time, until he was able to walk, in his slipper shaped cradle, strapped to his mother's back. When Ba-an-noce was particularly busy about her wigwam duties, setting up or taking down the teepee, her baby snugly wrapped in his cradle, would be dangling from the horn of his mother's saddle.

When He-des-tche-wa's baby days were over, he was his father's pride. Indians are very indulgent with their boys. While his little sisters were being brought up by their mother to assist with the various duties of the camp: cooking, gathering wood, dressing pelts and hides, making buckskin leggings and moccasins and learning shell work and beadwork, He-des-tche-wa would be allowed to pass his time unrestrained. He scampered around the camp, riding, fishing and hunting birds and other small game with his bow and arrows. He was only waiting for the time when he too would be old enough to ride out with the war party, a plumed and painted young brave.

The first incident of importance that Mr. Coolidge could remember took place when he was very small. The Arapahoes had pitched their teepees on the banks of a stream somewhere in Central Wyoming. The weather was fine, the camp was quiet, the men lounged in the shade, and children were playing close by. Only the women were busy about their work. Without the slightest warning, a great band of warriors charged through the camp, shooting and killing. Before the Arapahoes recovered from their surprise, the enemy had galloped out of sight. Nothing was left for them to do but care for the wounded and bury the dead.

Sherman Coolidge, First Arapahoe Episcopalian Priest

Soon after, the tribe had another bitter experience. The United States troops were in the field against the Sioux. An Arapahoe who was in the pay of the government, led them by mistake against his own people. The Arapahoes, on the march, were again taken by surprise and a great many of them were killed, including several of Mr. Coolidge's relatives. He escaped, as on the former occasion. Of course the soldiers expressed their regret for the mistake, then moved on. The Arapahoes have never forgiven the scout for his blunder. Though he was a very good man he was ostracized and shunned as a traitor ever after.

When He-des-tche-wa was about seven years old, he lost his father. Van-nas-du-hut left the main body of the Arapahoes, camped on the Big Horn River in Wyoming, and moved up on one of its tributaries on a hunting trip. In the evening he pitched his teepee in the bushes that grew on the river bank. At dusk he noticed a party of Indians killing a buffalo on a neighboring hill. Thinking they were friends, he apprehended no danger. Later that night however, his family was wakened by the fierce war whoops of Shoshones and Bannocks who had surrounded the camp. All ran for their lives and, under cover of darkness, got away except Van-nas-du-hut. He had remained at the camp to hold back the enemy while his family escaped. He-des-tche-wa, with the others, reached the main camp of the Arapahoes safely. The next morning a detail of warriors went back in search of Van-nas-du-hut. They found him lying dead, shot through the chest while defending his people.

After about two more years of free, wild life on the prairie, when He-des-tche-wa was nine years old, the Arapahoes moved into the Wind River country and camped on the confluence of the Wind River and the Popo Agie some miles below Camp Brown. He-des-tche-wa, his mother, a few old people and some children left their camp to go up to Camp Brown when a band of Bannocks and Shoshones, the hereditary foes of the Arapahoes, charged down upon them.[43] Their only chance for safety was to find concealment in the woods by the river. Even so they were soon discovered. Again He-des-tche-wa escaped with his life. When the Shoshones planned to kill him saying, "Look at his scalp lock, he is old enough to shoot us with an arrow." Gana-wea, a Shoshone himself but a

---

[43] *The Bates battle described here, named after Capt. A.E. Bates, occurred in 1874 on Nowood Creek at Paint Rock.*

man who had been employed for some time as a government scout said, "No," and he put the boy up on the horse with him.

One old man who had accompanied the little party was shot down while begging for his life. The others would probably have shared his fate had not some soldiers at the post observed the disturbance and gone to the scene. The prisoners were rescued and taken to Camp Brown where they remained under the protection of the garrison. Some of the officers wanted to save the little Indian boys in the party from their life of constant peril. After a good deal of persuasion, Ba-an-noce consented to part with He-des-tche-wa, his little brother, Ne-net-cha and his cousin, Cow-a-hay, knowing that they would be well cared for and protected by the Whites. Ne-net-cha-was taken by Lieutenant. Larabee, Cow-a-hay by Captain Russell and He-des-tche-wa by Dr. Sharpleigh. Captain and Mrs. Coolidge later adopted He-des-tche-wa and took him into their home. They took deep interest in the boy and brought him up with devoted attention and care. While in New York, Mrs. Coolidge had him baptized by Bishop Southgate at Zion Church. His early education was in Bishop Whipple's School in Faribault, Minnesota. He was eventually given the degree of Bachelor of Divinity at Seabury Divinity School in June, 1884. In the same year he was ordained to the deaconate by Bishop Whipple and was advanced to the priesthood by Bishop Spalding in 1885. He was sent to Fort Washakie, Wyoming, located fifteen miles from what had been Camp Brown, now the site of Lander; the place where he was captured and then rescued by the Shoshone, Gana-wea and the White soldiers. On the Reservation, he was to work as a Missionary to his own people who were then sharing the land with their old enemies, the Shoshones.

Ba-an-noce was still living and she had not forgotten her son. She was told of his expected arrival and every evening she would walk out to the road to meet the stage which would bring him back. Through unexpected delays, he was long in coming. Then one day he did come, this "White-man-Arapahoe." The Rev. John Roberts, who had arrived at the Shoshone Indian Agency the year before, tells of the meeting of the young clergyman with his mother. Ba-an-noce had last seen her He-des-tche-wa as a wild Indian boy, nine years old. Fourteen long years had elapsed since that time. There, a few paces in front of her, stood a tall stalwart, refined looking man. Shading her eyes with her hand, she cast a hurried glance toward him which was enough for a mother's eye. The old woman, bent down with the weight of age and affliction, went tottering

Sally Coolidge, daughter of Sherman and Grace Coolidge

toward him, then with a bound and a heart rending cry, she rushed to his arms. Relatives and kinfolk followed, each in turn, "fell on his neck and wept."

Ba-an-noce has long since left this 'vale of woe' to join little Ne-net-che and Cow-a-hay in the home where "the wicked cease from troubling and the weary are at rest." The Rev. John Roberts wrote of his native Arapahoe clergyman, "I was associated with the Rev. Sherman Coolidge in the church work on the Shoshone Indian Reservation and became intimately acquainted. For many years I lived under the same roof with him. During that time I never knew him to say an unkind word to anyone or to speak unkindly of anyone, though he was a man of strong feelings. I never knew him, in all those years, to do an ungentlemanly act."

Through Bishop Talbot's family, Mr. Coolidge met Miss Grace Weatherbee of New York City. He interested her in missionary work in Wyoming. She came out to the Reservation where she lived for a short time in a little cottage on the Shoshone Mission grounds, built for her by Mr. Roberts. In 1902 the Rev. Sherman Coolidge and Grace Weatherbee were married. They made their home at his ranch on his allotment near the Arapahoe camp. Of their own four children only two lived to grow up, with homes and families of the their own. Rev. and Mrs. Coolidge also suffered the loss of a little Arapahoe boy whom they adopted.

With his devoted wife, the Rev. Sherman Coolidge engaged in effective church work among his own people on the Reservation.[44]

---

[44] *The first part of this sketch of the early life of the Rev. Sherman Coolidge was written by the Rev. John Roberts about 1893, when he and Mr. Coolidge were working with the Arapahoe and Shoshone Indians on the Wind River Reservation. A copy of this account was published July 9, 1893, in* A Round Robin to the Junior Auxiliary. *The account here is given as it was originally written in 1893.*

Sherman Coolidge was a family friend when he lived on the reservation. He would often accompany us on family picnics and entertain us in the evening around the campfire with tales of his early life and adventures. He was a full-blooded Arapahoe, yet spent his young adulthood aspiring to become an Episcopal clergyman among White people.

Many years after Sherman Coolidge had left the Reservation and had gone to the Indian Territory in the Southern part of the United States, he and his wife returned to our home for a visit. I was very impressed with the beautiful silver jewelry that Coolidge's daughters, Rosebud and Sally, now grown young women, were wearing.

I was young at the time and didn't realize that the Coolidges were rather a unique family. Grace Coolidge had come from a very wealthy family. She had been a debutante in the East. Sherman, as a clergyman, was living in a very rustic type of shelter, with none of the luxuries that his bride had been accustomed to. She couldn't even converse with his Arapahoe relatives.

Soon after Bishop Nathaniel S. Thomas was elected the Bishop of Wyoming in 1909, he appointed the Rev. Sherman Coolidge a canon of St. Matthew's Cathedral, Laramie, Wyoming. Later Mr. Coolidge moved to Colorado where he became an honorary canon of St. John's Cathedral, Denver, a post which he held until his death. (He was once asked the meaning of 'canon.' He responded, "Big gun!")

Sherman Coolidge died in Los Angeles, January 24, 1932. He had gone to the coast a month before hoping to regain his health, which was failing. At the time of his death he was also rector of the Church of the Good Shepherd, Colorado Springs, Colorado.

Funeral of Washakie, Chief of the Shoshone Indians, died February 20, 1900. Rev. John Roberts and William McCabe standing on far side of caisson. Rev. Sherman Coolidge & Indian Agent Captain Nickerson, this side of caisson. Frank Allen, teamster, riding mule. The Indian raising the coffin in front of Nickerson, is Tigee, sergeant of Indian Scouts, Washakie's chief henchman. The Indian at his side is Tagwar, the one facing Tigee is Mal-ta-vish, all three Lemi or Salmon Eating Shoshones, kinsmen of Washakie, whose father was half Lemhi, half Flathead.
Lieutenant Overton, commanding officer at Fort Washakie at the time is seen on horseback between the heads of the two leading mules.

Chapter 4

Laura A. Roberts - by Beatrice Crofts

Much has been written about my maternal grandfather, John Roberts, the early friend and missionary to the Indians of the Wind River Reservation. Little has been written about his wife, my grandmother, Laura Alice Roberts. I would like to write down some of my memories, as I remember her, the things I remember her telling me, and the facts about her life that my mother recorded.[45]

~~~

My grandmother, Laura Alice Brown, was born in Nassau in 1864 of French and English ancestry. She had lived in Nassau on the Bahama Islands all of her young life. Her father was a very wealthy sponge merchant. He owned a fleet which employed natives to dive off of his ships into the ocean to bring up the sponges which were sold in the world markets. Laura Brown's grandfather had been born in Paris, and was sent to Nassau in the Bahama Islands as the French Consul.

My grandmother told me many pieces and bits of her childhood when I was young, and I didn't realize that she wouldn't always be here to repeat these stories. She never mentioned attending a school or a place where young children gathered to be educated, but did mention the many lessons she had with private tutors in her home. She did beautiful embroidery work, was fluent in French and had a very good musical education, something she used the rest of her life. Her life was very sheltered; she told me she had never been allowed to remain in the same room with a young gentleman or talk to one without the watchful company of an elder lady at all times. She had little patience with such guarded behavior but had no choice in the matter.

Laura Alice had never seen a cook stove in Nassau. The family meals were all prepared in a large room which was connected to their home by a long covered porch. All meals were carried in to the family and served at the proper time. My grandmother told me that the children were not allowed in this kitchen, in fact forbidden to go out there and bother

---

[45] *Portions reprinted from original publication in the* Wind River Mountaineer, *October-December 1985.*

Mrs. John Roberts, Laura Alice (Brown) Roberts. Photo taken in 1887.

the busy cooks. Perhaps this explains why she made a fire in the oven the first time that she was "on her own" and responsible for preparing a meal at the Wind River Indian Agency.

For entertainment, she and her brother swam in the ocean. They had a large heavy stone or brick wall in the back of their property, built to

Laura Alice Browns' home — Nassau, Bahama Islands -1800's

keep the ocean out of the yard. There was a large road on top of the wall where they could dive off into the ocean and swim, under the watchful eye of a guardian. Many years later, when with her grandchildren at Bull Lake, I remember our great astonishment when she joined us in the icy lake to demonstrate how to swim underwater. She swam a long distance and told us the water was nothing like the warm water at home.

Grandmama was seventeen years old and the organist at the cathedral in Nassau when John Roberts was first holding services. He had been sent to work among the lepers in some of the "outer islands," and was at the same time holding services at St. Matthew's Cathedral in Nassau. She met him at the church, and when he would come to call on her, she told me that they would sit on the veranda and visit, with her guardian rocking and sewing, between them. She was never allowed to visit alone or really become acquainted with John Roberts.

Laura and John visited in her home and at church but always in the presence of her governess or an older member of her family. They became engaged before he left the Bahama Islands.

When John Roberts reached the Indian Agency during the terrible blizzard of 1883 where the thermometer had fallen to sixty degrees below zero, he was living in a log building with the young Indian boys who were his pupils. With such primitive conditions, he wrote to Laura and asked her to break their engagement. He told her that he was living in such wild country that she would not survive if she came.

She replied that she was leaving Nassau and coming to the United States and the Indian Country by way of Liverpool. It was not clear when she would reach Rawlins, Wyoming territory. Rawlins was the nearest Union Pacific Railroad station.

Grandmama Laura had never seen snow. She had no knowledge of a Wyoming winter. She was utterly inexperienced in traveling by herself. But when the time came for her to leave her home and go to meet the man she had promised to marry, she started her journey.

Traveling by ship across the Atlantic, and then by train across most of the United States, was quite uncertain in those days. He could only guess when she would reach Rawlins. Roberts left the Reservation for Rawlins early on the morning of December 24, 1884. After a rough, cold ride of many hours on the stagecoach, over the snow covered hills, he arrived at his destination on the afternoon of Christmas Day. Grandmama had reached Rawlins early that same morning, after a 5,000 mile journey by sea and land.

It had been three years since they had seen each other and when they met at the hotel, she didn't recognize him. He was wearing a buffalo overcoat, a fur cap with ear muffs hiding much of his face, and thick Arctic boots, all covered with frost and snow. He little resembled the young clergyman in tropical "whites" to whom she had become engaged in Nassau.

They were married at four o'clock that day. It was the first wedding in Rawlins' new St. Thomas Episcopal church, an event recounted many times to family members. The Roberts were strangers in town, but the church was filled to capacity with friendly people to welcome them and to wish them well in their new life together. The name, Mrs. Roberts, was on a gift on the Christmas tree, but when it was called, she failed to react.

The next morning, they started the trip to the Reservation by stage, although the snow was deep and the cold still extreme. On the evening of the second day, they reached Lander where the driver had been instructed to take them to the home of Major Baldwin. He and his wonderful family gave them a warm welcome. The two days and a night of continuous traveling on a stage, stopping only for meals, had been very difficult.

The next stop after leaving Lander was their new home, one room in the old adobe boarding school at the Wind River Agency, known as the Government Industrial school. Grandmama told me that as the team topped the small hill and started down toward the Agency, she could see hundreds of small lights in the night. These were the campfires of the Indians camped around the agency.

It was a harsh environment in a new country with living conditions primitive beyond belief, but in the exuberance of her youth and young love, it was a wonderful and glorious country. She lived in a building shared with children and young adults of both the Shoshone and Arapahoe Tribes. The children knew nothing of the discipline or order of school life the White people were attempting to teach them. There was also the extreme cold of the Wyoming winters, the lack of social life, and a dearth of music and books. Even the mail, when it arrived, was many weeks old.

Laura missed the trees and flowers of her homeland, so when spring came to Wyoming, she planted many young trees and native wild flowers around the school building. The older Indian pupils were soon helping her transplant these. There were a few government employees living at the Agency and at Fort Washakie, about a mile and a half away. Here, at the fort, there were also officers and the men stationed to keep the peace and a few of these had brought their families with them.

Grandmama was a very small person. (She never reached her desired weight of 100 pounds.) Her rather stern and serious pictures do not show the real person I knew. I can imagine as I look at the photos, her comment, "Do not make me laugh. As the wife of a clergyman, I should have a serious and dignified demeanor."

Her photos do not reveal the fearless horsewoman who would often race her horse and frighten the family with her wild and unladylike exuberance. I remember the time a group of us rode into Louis Lake. We were camped at Granier Meadows and were leaving early that morning to go into the lakes to fish. This was many years before anyone had even talked about a road being built into the area. I was the youngest grandchild and had permission to accompany the adults, but being the youngest, I was given the doubtful (to me) privilege of being told to ride behind my grandmama. I complained bitterly to her that everyone would think that I was a baby riding behind her and to make matters worse, we were given an old white horse. In my eyes, he didn't look able to make the trip. I was still complaining when we took off. We loped ahead, only slowing once to pick our way across a swamp. I hung on, too busy keeping my back seat to complain anymore. We arrived at the lake first and Grandmama, turning to me said with a laugh, "Who will tease us for being the youngest or the eldest? We can ride like the wind."

I often spent the night with my grandparents at the Mission. They had a very small bedroom at the bottom of the stairs. I would stand at the bottom of the stairs and watch each school girl take off her shoes and place them in the hall. These shoes, all different sizes, were polished and placed in a neat row. I remember watching each of the older girls take up a lighted lamp and go up the stairs in single file to the two dormitories on the second floor. The halls were icy but the dormitories each had a wood or coal stove to take off the chill. I was allowed to watch this nightly procession, telling each girl goodnight before going into my grandparent's room.

In their room they had a small brass bed in which I slept. The room would be very cold around the edges, but warm if one stood close to the heating stove while getting ready for bed. In the night I would often wake up and hear the coyotes on the hills all around the Mission. That can be a lonely sound to a small child; I was not really convinced that the coyotes were not interested in coming any closer to the outbuildings.

I have told about my grandparent's bedroom because there is something of my grandmama's life in this; it was this room that held her life. In the early days of the school, when the other parts of the Mission were filled with Indians, weddings, baptisms, funerals, sickness, hunger, and troubles, this small bedroom was the only place that really belonged to Grandmama and that was set apart from her life as a missionary's wife. Here, she could just be herself and worry about the snowstorms coming over the Wind Rivers, rock a child, or tell stories about her life when she was small.

In the summer evenings we could sometimes sit on the porch and visit. Many times we would hear the beautiful soft sounds of the Indian flutes. To me the sound has never been equaled. It is beautiful but haunting music. Grandmama told me this was the music the young Indian men played when they went courting.

As a child I can never remember a door or a window being locked. This was to encourage Indian people to come and visit as they wished. When my grandmama first came to the Reservation, she told me how the Indians would pull blankets up behind their heads to help them see into the windows. They were interested in seeing how this strange White woman lived. She became accustomed to this and remarked how she missed their company when she was no longer of such keen interest to them.

After central heating was put into the Mission, my grandmother would go down to the cellar to check the old furnace and to make sure there was a plentiful supply of coal on hand. The cellar was a very mysterious place to me. If we would sit very close together and be very still, grandmother's "Old Mamma" cat would come out and so reveal the place where she had hidden her latest batch of kittens. I'm sure that "Old Mamma" must have had a thousand kittens. They were always carefully undisclosed until it was 'too late'. I was never sure just how late was 'too late'. I only knew that my grandmama always had small, warm kittens for me to hold.

Grandmama loved wild west movies. Perhaps this was because Tim McCoy was a frequent guest of the Roberts family, or perhaps the movies simply appealed to her because they showed a romantic, unrealistic way of life in the 'Wild West'. Anyway, she loved them. The owner of the Grand Theater in Lander gave her a lifetime pass in recognition of her many years of community service, but this created a problem. She wasn't sure a clergyman's wife should be seen sitting at the Saturday afternoon show every week. However, it would be thought perfectly acceptable if she had a small grandchild by the hand. Needless to say, I enjoyed this privilege for many years.

It was not considered seemly for an Episcopal clergyman to dance during the era that my grandparents lived. And grandmama loved to dance. Grandmama would dance all evening while my grandpapa would sit on the sidelines and visit with the army men, settlers, and their wives.

Laura Roberts was first and foremost a clergyman's wife. But she was also a person that I'm sure didn't always want to go to church, play the organ, have guild meetings and organize another Sunday school. She mentioned to me once that "Papa", as she called him, didn't always need to help the elderly women and assist the "good church ladies" down the street while she dealt with the mud puddles and broken board walks on her own.

Beside care of children and home, grandmama had many things to fill her days. There were churches some miles from the Agency where Sunday school classes were being organized, supervised and taught. At the boarding school she often filled in if one of the teachers became ill. One of the people that my grandmother held in high regard, for many good reasons, was the cook. There were many people to feed: the regular Indian children attending the school, the teachers, the matrons, parents, often visiting dignitaries, the visiting bishop with his family, the seven members of the Roberts family, and almost always people that came to the Mission just to visit and see Indians for themselves.

After she had filled in and taken over for many cooks over the years, she gained lots of experience but never a tremendous amount of knowledge. She did not love to cook.

The huge cook stove in the old Mission kitchen was high, with large lids almost too heavy for her to lift. As an added frustration, the fire box was far below the top of the stove. It was almost too much for her to cope with.

The many visiting grandchildren were not allowed to go in the kitchen or bother the cook in any way. "The cook may get on the stage and go home," was the dire threat often heard. Yes, my grandmama did respect the cook.

During her adult life, Grandmama had little privacy in her home, as it was always full of little Indian children. She had none of the modern conveniences as we know them today. I remember the great excitement when they got the Delco light plant. It made lots of noise when it ran, and each morning my grandmother took a pitcher of water inside the screen cage to fill a great number of things that looked like old automobile batteries. She had all of these chores to do because Grandpapa was away from home a great deal of the time.

My Grandparents could not afford any indoor plumbing until long after my grandmama died. They did have a hand pump in the kitchen that was a great help; it meant they no longer had to carry water from the creek. This must have been a tremendous chore, for every drop of water for all of the children to bathe in was carried, heated, and then poured into round tin tubs. The older girls helped the very small ones to bathe.

When the Roberts' first child was born, he lived only a few hours. They didn't talk much about him, but I do know that Grandmama was looking forward to this baby as a companion, someone to talk to. She was alone so much of the time that she must have felt very isolated. Even the distance to Lander was far by buggy or horseback. When the baby died, he was buried in the military cemetery just west of the fort. Today, the baby's grave is marked by a small, moss covered stone just to the north of the large stone marking Chief Washakie's grave.

I thought of having it moved to the cemetery in Lander. The baby's grave seems so lonely, but this small White child belongs there. He is surrounded by the Indian's graves and the old graves of the early soldiers. He was a part of that early time in Wyoming — the happiness, the work, the trials, and the sadness. These are all a part of the coming of the first missionary to the land of the Indians — the land of the "Warm Valley" and the shining Mountains. The infant son of John and Laura Roberts was left there because we know he lies among friends on the Reservation.

Grandmama spent many long and lonely hours. Grandpapa was a busy and dedicated man, and his work took him many miles from home each day. He visited the Indian camps, helped the poor and the hungry, buried the dead, held weddings and baptized babies. He started churches in Lander, Milford, Dubois, Thermopolis, Shoshoni and Hudson, Riverton, Wind River Agency, the Shoshone Mission, Ethete, and held services in Atlantic City, South Pass, Crowheart, Lyons Valley and Circle.

The guest book at the Shoshone Mission contains the names of visitors from all over the world. Some of these names are illustrious, some are not. In the early days of the Mission, these visitors came on horseback and in covered wagons and some walked. A number would have to stay overnight at least. Later they came in cars, and there were many of them interested in seeing the Mission and in hearing about the work being done there. They took pictures of the little pupils, those who could be persuaded to face the camera after being bribed and coaxed to come from under the table or from behind the door. With few exceptions, the visitors walked through the orchard, on the cobblestone path, to spend a few minutes in the Chapel of the Holy Saints John.

Some of these visitors may have decided to keep a diary of all the places they visited, since as soon as everyone was comfortably seated in the offices or on the porch, very business-like notebooks were taken out. "Now, Dr. Roberts, we would like a history of chief Washakie, the story of Sacajawea, the Shoshone girl guide with the Lewis and Clark Expedition and a sketch of your life here. And would you hurry please, we have only a short time." So many times the visitor would inquire of Mr. Roberts why he didn't write a book telling of his experiences in living and working for so many years on the Indian Reservation. His answer was a very true one — "If I take the time to stop and write there will be nothing to write."

Conclusion

At the conclusion of her memoirs, my mother, Elinor Markley, wrote the following:

When the Shoshone Mission was first established, there was not a farm nor field in sight. Now it is surrounded by farms and homes. Since the Rev. John Roberts began his wonderful ministry to the Indians, in 1883, they are a completely different people. This great change can be seen in their family life, in their relations with each other and with the White people, whether friend or employer. They appreciate all the conveniences and comforts and privileges of civilized life. They no longer live in fear and terror of "Nin-im-be" and other evil influences.

For sixty-six years Dr. John Roberts carried on his faithful ministry to the Arapahoes and Shoshones and among the White settlers within a radius of one hundred miles of Shoshone Agency. On horseback or with his team and buckboard, he visited all the churches he had established. Very little money was forthcoming for church work and too often the program had to be modified according to the available resources.

In 1932, the Rev. John Roberts was given an honor of distinction at the University of Wyoming commencement when Dr. A.G. Crane conferred upon him the honorary degree of Doctor of Laws, the first recognition of this kind that the institution had ever made. At the close of the ceremonies, conferring degrees upon the members of the senior class, President Crane, in a brief address, said, "Rev. John Roberts, in recognition of your untiring efforts as a teacher, of the courage you have evidenced in pioneering important work within the boundaries of our great state, for your perseverance and success in these efforts, I have the honor to confer on you the highest degree which this institution can offer. I now confer upon you the degree of Doctor of Laws with all the rites and privileges there unto appertaining here or elsewhere." The great audience rose to its feet to cheer this pioneer missionary and his wife and to accord to him the honor so justly his due.

In the same year, my mother continued, the Western Theological Seminary, Evanston, Illinois, conferred upon the Rev. John Roberts the degree of Doctor of Divinity, Honoris Causa, "in recognition of his long and faithful ministry as a missionary among the Indians and White settlers of Wyoming and of his translations of portions of the Bible and Book of Common Prayer, into the Arapahoe and Shoshone language."

Other honors she noted include one in 1933 when the State Legislature of Wyoming adopted a "Resolution of Appreciation of fifty years of invaluable and unparalleled service rendered to their Church, Community, State and Nation by Dr. and Mrs. John Roberts."

Dr. Roberts was again honored a year later, on February 26, when the Wyoming state flag was presented in the great choir of the National Cathedral in Washington, "In appreciation of the nation for his work of fifty years in missionary endeavor among the Shoshone and Arapahoe Indians and the White settlers adjacent to the Wind River Reservation. The extraordinary useful and helpful service of Dr. Roberts to the Indians and Whites alike, aided by his faithful wife, are gratefully appreciated by the people of Wyoming as evidenced by a resolution of appreciation adopted by the Legislature of Wyoming, February 14, 1934. We honor our state by recognizing these distinguished services in the presentation of this flag."

The presentation of the flag was made by Mrs. Mondell in the name of Wyoming citizens, at the suggestion of Senator Robert D. Carey and by the endorsement of the former congressman, Frank W. Mondell. It had been the custom, for each state to present its state flag to the National Cathedral in honor of its most distinguished citizen. These flags were to be preserved and displayed permanently in the Cathedral in Washington.

Epilogue
by Beatrice Crofts

Life on the Reservation

My father, Charles Markley, was the bookkeeper for the J.K. Moore Indian Trading company. We lived in a huge house which had been built by J.K. Moore, Sr. The ceilings were twelve feet high and it had fourteen rooms with windows that reached to the floor. These were beautiful but were very cold during the Wyoming winters of thirty below zero. The house was too large for our family of four, but we and the Ansells, with their five children, shared it. This was a delightful arrangement for the children, because five children through one closed door, added much to the drama and excitement of our daily lives. We had one spare back bedroom which was always kept ready for Jim Moore, the son of J.K. Moore, Sr., when he came to spend time at the fort.

In summer Jim Moore's family often came from California. We would play in a shed that had stacks of buffalo hides piled up, almost to the roof. The buffalo hides stored in the old "Red Shed" behind our home at Fort Washakie were old and forgotten. I do not know, or have knowledge of anyone who may remember how these were ever disposed of. They were stiff and seemed to be bailed together. They were not the cleanest things to play on. There was also an old army ambulance that perhaps had been left behind when the Post was abandoned. This had a few tattered curtains that would flutter in the wind. We had many Indian fights and battles from this ambulance; sometimes we were the Indians and sometimes the soldiers. We had hay stacks to slide down, and corrals full of cattle to ride and rope. Our summers were always full.

Jim Moore's middle daughter, Barbara, Mrs. Frederick Fish, Jr. of Dubois, and I became friends. We were about the same age and we each owned an Indian pony. This gave us freedom to travel all over the countryside. One summer there was great excitement throughout the fort. Movie stars had come to make a film and there was going to be a fort and large Indian camp built in South Fork Canyon. Barbara and I were discussing this great event as we sat on our horses one summer morning. We heard a bugle blowing and a great number of soldiers on horses caught

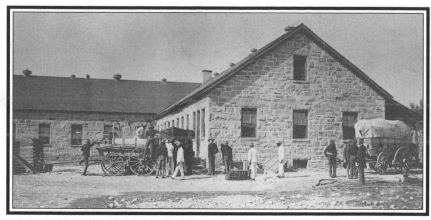

Soldiers at old Fort Washakie barracks. This view is facing south.

up with us on the road. The group halted and the officer in charge asked us which road would take them to South Fork. This was the U.S. Cavalry from the area! Without a moment's hesitation, we offered to lead them! The flag was waving, the bugle softly blowing and we were riding ahead of the troop. I have never been in a position where I felt so important. Barbara will always be the friend who shared that moment in history. We guided the U.S. Cavalry to the great Indian Battle on the South Fork of the Little Wind! I didn't realize that these troops knew all of the roads and trails in the area until years later, and then, it didn't matter!

The first house I remember at the Fort was placed in the middle of the parade ground. This was a huge white house that resembled the White House. When I was very small I thought that God lived there, but when I was older I knew that the Indian Agent lived there. I couldn't understand why the Indians had an Agent that couldn't even speak Shoshone or Arapahoe as my grandparents and my parents could. It was at this same house that many of the families were invited for an evening of tea and cake. The Agent had a prized possession — a radio! It was a great excitement to have a chance to hear the new invention! We had tea and cake and then each person was given the opportunity to put on the headphones and hear the voice. When my turn came I sat there and listened, and listened and listened! I looked at the circle of expectant guests waiting to see the great reaction on the face of a child. I heard nothing! I was desperate, so I lied to the group, "It is wonderful!"

The store at the Fort had hitching racks; rows of them to the west side of the building. Every morning when it was about time for the stage to bring the mail, the Indians arrived. The wagons, with their iron wheels, protesting at the bitter cold, would come squeaking with agony across the snow packed road. Men, women and children would climb out of the open lumber wagons and go into the store. A few younger men would ride up shouting and running to show off their horsemanship. Where the door opened into the store, there was a large room with shelves and show cases along the sides. In the middle was a great wood and coal stove with a coal bucket sitting near it. Around this stove were placed a dozen or more odds and ends of chairs where all of the men sat down. It was quiet when they first arrived, and they were content to be there and enjoy the warmth, a smoke and quiet companionship. The many times I walked into the store, I never saw an Indian lady sitting in one of these chairs. That's just the way it was. The women with cradle boards on their backs and usually a small child by the hand were busy making a few purchases. In the back of the store was a large round cheese, perhaps two or three feet in diameter. They would buy a small slice of cheese, a few soda crackers in the bulk and perhaps a little coffee or a small sack of flour. They had very little money but some would have a few precious beaded belongings to trade. We had very little but the Indians had even less.

When I was about nine or ten years old, the Rural Electric Authority (REA) came to the Reservation. This great improvement in our lives consisted of one light bulb hung down in the center of each room. It made a great difference in our lives — we didn't have to crowd around one small kerosene lamp like moths at night to sew or read. For many years, my father had read the old classics aloud to us as my mother sewed. We were allowed to stay up and listen and now we had a better light for our only evening entertainment. I had listened to the stories of Thackeray, De Voto, Dickens and Hugo before I learned to read.

Each winter our water pipes would freeze. We had one faucet in the back yard, which, if left running all of the time, would not freeze up. This was great. It made a skating rink in our back yard, but in turn, this made it more difficult to get near with a bucket to fill with water. The walking was hazardous; we had many buckets of water to carry into the house after school. Water had to be heated on the stove each night and baths had to be taken even if the temperature was just a little above freezing in the bathroom. Our house was not warm. I owned three school dresses and they were all scorched in the back from backing up too close to the stove.

My sister and I went to the rural school. One teacher would ride horseback from her ranch about two miles away. When she arrived, late many times, she would be dreadfully cold. It was her duty to start a fire in the stove and try to get each child and herself a little warmer before starting our lessons. We usually had about forty pupils crowded into one room with all eight grades included. Many of the children attended this rural school rather than attending the BIA boarding school. Our teacher usually read to us until about noon because it was too cold in the room for us to leave the space around the stove and "take our seats." After lunch she would work with the little ones, attempting to teach them to read by using texts about the average middle class White family, stories that had no meaning or anything in common to most of the group.

The District School

When I entered first grade, I walked across the back yard, crawled through the barbed wire and was on the school ground. Our teacher taught us first by reading a chart. We all stood in a circle and she pointed to this chart and read the words to us. This was the way it was done. The other children in this circle were Indians and I was, at this time, the only White. Many of these little Indians could not speak a word of English. The family of the chart was the typical White family. Their home was a house, not a tent, the father went off to work each morning, and the mother made beds and cooked. I am sure that no Indian father at that time went off each morning to work at the office. I am sure that no Indian mother stood in her home and prepared delicious meals at a kitchen sink. This typical family did not apply to any of my classmates. I am sure they thought these people lived on Mars.

As I progressed through the grades with my same classmates, we learned all sorts of useful things! I can remember one of the Indian boys and I sitting near each other and being drilled on the names of cattle breeds. When I reached grade four, the teacher decided that I was brilliant; this was because I could speak the language in which our books were written! I had a little background because my parents owned books so I skipped the grade where pupils were usually taught multiplication tables and other necessary things. I learned to add fast but couldn't quite keep up with the other children who had learned their tables in the town school. Each year I just had to work a little faster to make up for the schooling I had missed because I excelled in reading compared to my Indian friends. My teachers simply didn't seem to realize that I had a tremendous advantage in learning to read the chart and could progress very quickly because I already spoke the English language.

As we progressed through the grades, we did have other White children joining us in school. Sometimes the White government employees would have children that were still in grade school, and the Ansell children were in school with us until they moved to Wind River and entered school there.

We had many different teachers through the years. At the time, I didn't realize it but those teachers must have had a dreadful job. They were glad for any kind of a job then; the pay was low and the job tremendous, but the majority of these young women had worked hard most of their lives.

One of our early teachers in the District School on the Reservation was Vincoe Charity Mushrush. When she left the school district, she completed nurse's training and was sent to China in 1937 by the Christian Missionary Society to work as a nurse near Shanghai.

We seldom had a teacher who was able to speak Shoshone or Arapahoe. The older children would have long assignments written out on the board. I was always wishing that the hundreds of papers that I handed in would be checked or graded. The teacher, of course, had no time for papers or suggestions. She was fortunate to just get by each day. I did learn to read to myself for hours but I had large gaps in my education that could not all be filled by reading.

~~~

The following article, taken from the *Casper Star Tribune,* seems to me to provide a fitting epilogue for my mother's memories:

The Wind River Reservation seems to be well provided with churches and schools, St. Stephen's and Ethete as well as several other church buildings — but the original Mission established by the late Dr. John Roberts, Episcopal missionary who devoted 66 years to the Indians, has been abandoned.

The grounds, once well irrigated and tended, are growing to weeds, but there are still flowers, growing wild now, in what once were flower beds, and the apple trees keep on bearing fruit. It is an historical and lovely sight in a grove of great trees and seems to deserve a better fate.

This was written in 1963. Since then many other changes have taken place. There are three churches on the Mission grounds. The old Mission building is crumbling down but has been placed on the National Historical Register. The hand laid cobblestones have all been removed from the path going to the chapel. Many of the fruit trees are gone but this is still a beautiful site.

During the early evening hours of spring, you can go back in time, listen and imagine the young men playing soft plaintive songs on their flutes, hear again the soft beating of the drum coming from the teepees east of the Mission and perhaps the old Mission bell calling the little Indian children into Vesper service. You might even hear John Roberts saying, "No, I will never leave my people, they will need me always!"

The site that Washakie chose for his people is still beautiful, and as Washakie said to John Roberts when he gave him this land, "The hope of our people is in the children. They must be educated in the new ways for the survival of our tribe in the coming generations."

When I was looking through the rich collection of papers, letters and stories written by my grandfather, I found this old poem that he had composed so many years ago. I tried to lay it aside and forget about it, but found that it has a haunting and unforgettable theme running through it. As I read it, I remembered that many times he took me on his lap when I was small and told me about his mother and his home in Wales. He talked a great deal about his mother and after I read many of his old letters, I felt that her influence was very strong in his life. He wanted to study medicine and become a doctor. His mother wanted him to become a clergyman so he became a clergyman.

Perhaps through this poem, written before he left his homeland, he realized that it would be very difficult to return. When he was sent to the West Indies he worked among the lepers. He told his superiors in the church that most of these people were Christians and that he wished for more difficult work. They complied and sent him to the Shoshone and Bannock Reservation. When he came to the Reservation he had to make a complete new life for himself. I wonder if he looked back at his "Isle of Beauty?" Never in all of my years of visiting with him, listening to him visit with other people, or in going through all of his old records, did he ever show any regrets for his chosen life. He loved the Indians and fought each day for the betterment of their lives and future. He did apply for a transfer to Africa at one time early in his career, thinking a warmer climate

there would benefit Laura Alice, his wife, because it would be more like
the climate of her "West Indies." The church refused to let him go.

I wonder if my mother, who so carefully copied all of Grandfather's
materials, also read this poem, and if so perhaps tried to discover in it a
glimpse of John Roberts' future rather than just the musings of a young
school boy, lost for a moment:

Isle of Beauty

In the hour when happy faces
Smile around the taper light,
Who will fill our vacant places
Who will sing our songs to-night?
What would I not give to wander
Where my old companions dwell,
Absence makes the heart grow fonder
Isle of Beauty fare thee well.
Shades of evening close not o'er us
Leave our lonely bark awhile,
Morn alas will not restore us
Yonder dim and distant isle.
Still my fancy can discover
Sunny spots where friends may dwell,
Darker Shadows round us hover
Isle of Beauty fare thee well.

Poem written 1869
by John Roberts, age 16
Rutlin Grammar School

Illustration by
Tom Lucas

Census Roll

Shoshone and Bannock Agency, Wyoming Territory, October 8, 1877

Lodge	M	W	C	Name
1	5	3	2	Fah-woo-yag-gi
2	1	3	2	Fish-sho-give-na-e
3	3	2	5	To-gwut-te-a
4	4	5	3	Ho-wat-se
5	1	3	1	Nah-ro-rah-ke
6	2	3	4	Ash-we-yah
7	1	1	0	Qut-tah-not-sone
8	1	3	1	Mo-hau-uimp-e-kah
9	2	2	1	No-Hoit
10	1	2	2	No-yo-se
11	3	5	2	Ne-vah
12	4	3	1	Ho-nah-hit-se
13	2	2	1	Kip-pehal-or-han
14	1	2	2	Le-via
15	1	2	4	Wit-tom-bony
16	1	3	1	Ah-vite-se
17	2	2	0	Te-he-u-do-go
18	1	3	4	Tap-paa
19	2	4	1	O-na-u-goo-schic
20	4	3	1	To-dzan-na
21	1	2	1	Toyah-git-tsah-tsah-pah
22	1	1	3	Se-ah-no
23	2	2	3	Gan-ah-wunts
24	1	2	1	Woug-bo-dzock-ah
25	1	0	2	Zony (Indian woman)
26	1	2	3	Ba-ha-goo-sha
27	0	1	1	Mary Reese
28	1	2	3	Gau-ny
29	1	1	2	Ke-wim-bassa
30	12	1	1	Ta-ahar-rah
31	1	1	1	Pap-pag-go wot
32	3	2	1	Ah-ren-ap-way
33	1	1	1	To, Coutch
34	2	5	2	Une-ty-bo
35	5	3	1	A-go-nar-a-cop
36	1	3	4	Ta-go-i-tah
37	4	2	5	Tse-goom-bah

38	1	1	3	Ge-ge-bo
39	2	2	3	Tab-be-shwot
40	3	2	2	Swa-m-poy
41	1	1	3	Ni-yo-go-n do-go
42	1	2	4	No-go-ho-go
43	2	3	3	Wan-ny-bitz (chief)
44	3	2	3	Per-rau
45	2	2	2	O-hah-tah chief
46	5	5	6	Wash-a-kie,head chief
47	2	3	0	Po-nau-vish-u-rah, chief
48	3	3	0	Sho-pahk-ha-ma
49	0	2	2	Ten-e-mau-ka-wat
50	1	2	2	Pah-gau-dzon-nu-w-haw-it
51	1	2	4	Peh-hah-ro-ho-ri
52	2	2	2	Tash-gore
53	3	3	2	Pah-gau-it-se
54	4	1	0	Wer-ven-gow, chief
55	1	1	2	Pah-ho-no-ho
56	1	1	2	Ba-by
57	3	2	5	I-den-hi-nut
58	2	3	2	Wau-nah-moo-se-wah
59	3	1	4	Ty-bo-ro-se-do
60	1	3	3	Pah-dzoi-gwit-tah
61	2	1	3	Te-rau-got-se
62	1	4	5	Pah-gwe-nump
63	1	2	3	Nash-e-wich-e
64	2	1	2	Nar-kok, chief
65	2	3	2	En-gah-tome
66	2	3	4	Fa-goon-dum, chief
67	2	2	1	Ten-ap-way
68	1	2	3	Ou-dau-bo-ra-se
69	4	2	2	To-tam-mah
70	1	1	4	Moon-in-hab-be
71	1	2	2	Ta-wo-e-bit-se
72	3	3	5	George Washington
73	3	3	2	We-saw
74	1	1	1	Nag-ga-ro-ny
75	2	2	1	Fred-e-vick
76	3	2	3	Riv-vau-in-dzah-se-nah
77	1			Tah-vas
78	3	1	0	Tse-go-vi-a
79	1	1	6	To-nam-be

80	2	3	2	Seg-we-no
81	3	4	3	Tse-conts
82	1	2	1	O-shah-vite-se
83	1	1	1	Won-se-ah
84	5	3	1	En-gah-timp
85	2	2	2	Ah-n-guit-tah
86	2	4	2	Ish-n-quash
87	1	1	6	Mo-vo
88	1	4	1	Pah-shup
89	1	2	1	Hodzah-tse
90	1	1	1	Wooug-gunt
91	1	0	1	Ho-to-go
92	2	1	1	Ah-bish-she-ga
93	1	3	3	Wo-too-sah-nah
94	1	1	3	Ish-i-yuh
95	1	2	3	Ho-i-go-iwhe-de
96	1	1	2	Pah-ho-mo-nidit-se
97	1	2	3	Git-sa-vah
98	1	3	4	Fish-ah-wuck-ko
99	2	2	1	Ne-hah
100	2	2	2	To-gi-yag-gi
101	1	2	1	Ho-guash-sho
102	2	2	3	Mas-se-wo-go-nat-se
103	3	3	1	Ten-ah-pit-ey
104	0	1	0	Coo-dze-noo-ah
105	1	2	2	Co-va-vah-saht
106	1	2	3	To-shag-quash-n´dim-me
107	1	1	3	Tah-ne-tsit-tse
108	1	2	1	Jim
109	2	2	2	Toop-se-po-wot, chief
110	1	2	1	Shar-ro-weetz
111	11	11	2	Tah-to-it-se
112	2	2	3	Shon-dit-se
113	3	4	1	Bat-tez
114	1	1	0	Mah-ve-sip
115	1	1	4	Hi-bun-do-sah
116	4	1	1	Andrew
117	3	2	1	*Bazil, chief*
118	0	3	0	*Bazil's Mother*
119	2	2	3	Beaver, Chatey
120	1	1	0	Ha-ue-whep
121	1	2	2	Hi-vo-wah

122	1	2	0	So-phia
123	1	1	0	Dje-shah-wuh
124	2	3	0	Sho-ne-dze-gwe-ah
125	2	1	3	Wau-dat-se
126	3	2	2	Tse-kah-nah-ve-te
127	1	4	0	Po-ue-wun-nah
128	1	1	4	Ah-u´-do-o-ah
129	3	3	2	Wo-wim-boouk
130	2	1	1	Wagon Jim
131	1	2	2	Pau-gwo-dzo-ne
132	2	2	2	Wah-hou-wuh
133	2	2	5	Om-be-ship
134	1	2	1	Shoyoh
135	1	2	3	John Sin-clare
136	1	2	0	Ah-wun
137	1	1	4	U-tah
138	2	3	3	Naa-kie
139	1	2	4	Quin-date-se
140	2	2	2	Ho-ah-ri
141	1	2	0	Nah-wuut-se
142	1	1	2	Sah-vo-vi-yah
143	1	1	3	Ah-git-se
144	3	2	0	Mo-dzump
145	1	2	1	Pesh-it-se
146	1	1	2	Ko-ro-ke
147	2	4	2	Mo-hah-vo-kah
148	2	2	1	Pe-ah-en-gah
149	2	1	0	Mo-mo
150	1	3	0	Gwuh-not
151	0	1	3	En-gah-dwot-se
152	1	1	0	Tis-sa-vit-tah
153	3	2	2	To-ash-u-ah
154	2	2	0	Ne-me-ra-gwot-se
155	2	2	1	To-ne-boonk
156	1	2	5	Meh-dzah-tse
157	0	1	3	Julia
158	2	3	3	Shaw-wun-vit-se
159	1	1	0	Tape-sau-e-vit-te
160	3	2	3	Pe-te-o-ge
161	4	4	3	Wo-bit-se
162	0	2	3	Wobit-se II
163	4	3	1	Sar-i-at

164	0	2	1	Julia C.
165	1	1	3	Louis Leclare
166	1	2	0	Edmo Leclare
167	1	1	1	Quit-tam-be
168	0	1	1	John's Wife
169	1	1	1	Toon-ya-vis-sa
170	0	1	3	Ola-ho
171	3	4	1	Weatch
172	2	2	2	Shar-a-gaut
173	0	1	6	Kossuth's wife
174	0	3	3	Tra-he-oo's wife

Shoshone group (Brush tipi in rear is for shade) circa 1860, South Pass

The following pages are the Arapahoe then the Shoshone Vocabularies which John Roberts labored over with the help of his Indian friends.

Arapahoe Vocabulary

alone .... na-ne-se
among the trees .... hau-haudee
Arapahoe .... he nau nau a nau (Crow word meaning "the tattooed")
bacon .... nuh-thi-uh-ah
bear .... wuch
beautiful .... he thet ne au
big water .... va na sau neje
bright spring .... he jan vaa hau cha vin na
candle .... nw the yu
candy .... chay na
cedar .... va tha nau au
coffee .... we ti u
cold .... nw go tha
cow .... wa cutch
come .... na hi tch
contentment .... hau wu ne au
creator .... he jav a ne au thau
dime .... nicka-naysa
dog .... ath a ve or ja a
earth .... ve dau au wu
elk .... wu chu
far off .... va va on
fire (camp) .... he sed a
fire (sage) .... nau casis
fishing place .... na de nau nau yau ne
five cents .... Nock-yoo
flat .... ja je da yau
food .... vet hee de
fragrant .... ne e vau au
friendship .... he ne dau e va de de
girl .... iss say
green foliage .... ja na da ne gau
gum .... chi ava chay na
happiness .... hau nau wu tha jau ha de de
hat .... wad e
heaven .... he ja va a
hillside .... ha cha vee

him .... nun na nyn
hog .... ne au tha wuch
horse .... wu chu auch
house of many rooms .... wau nau thae jae chau hau wuu
hunting place .... na de nau a de ne
I .... nun a nu
ice .... wau ua wa
idleness .... thau nu hu dein the meadow... ja ne thau
incense .... ja a
in the meadow .... ja ne thau
in the woods .... hau hau dee
island .... ba na a
it is enough .... na adau chee
long view .... va va on nau hau thae
match .... wa tot
many birds .... hau wu hu ne ha he hau
marsh .... thau asa na yau
milk .... beth en netch
moon .... ve gu ne se
mountain .... hau ane
mountain sheep .... hod de
mutal love .... ve chu tha de de
no .... e ka
no good .... wah sah
on a cliff .... jau uu da
on a shore .... ses thau wu
our home .... ha ya in
place to eat .... na da ve the he dau ne
place to rest .... na da dau ya nu se na
pleasant .... ne au
prairie .... he thau wu u
quarter .... che va ny
rocky place .... hau nau hau nau ga ne ne
rest .... dau yu nu see
sandy .... nun au vae ne
slave .... wau wau nau
snow .... hee
stars .... hau thau u
stillness .... da ne da yau
stove .... jatch then
stranger on high .... he je va ne a tha
sugar .... nah sio cha
summer .... ve jane
sun .... he se se

tobacco .... si sa wa ista
victory .... hau e a de
water.. netch
when friends meet......................... ne dau au ae sa the he ne dae hau au
when the wind blows .... na dau sae sa
when the birds sing.. ne dau nea hee
when the family meets .... na dan ae sa the
where two roads cross .... nau gau chu van nau
you .... xnun a ni

Numbers

one .... ne sa te
two .... ne se
three .... nas a
four .... yane e
five .... yah tha ne
six .... ne tha

Translated in 1889 by Rev. John Roberts, D.D.LL.D
Assited by Fremont Arthur, his Arapahoe Indian pupil, 1883-1897

Phonetic Translations of Prayers in the Arapahoe Language

The Lord's Prayer

Heesjeva hene Sunauneet; Heneseet vedenau; Nuchaja honoit haithauka hinona. Haithet honoit nauvedaw, hasau heesjeva. Jevenaa nuhw desene vethewa. Jeva gaudauvanadau desnundaun, as jegaudauvanawneua wchadaunau...Jevaethaaitcthaa hada ethete, Heseevahee Hesunaunin, Nevahaistaut detcanehe. Hoiee.

The Apostles' Creed

Nethauwadanau Hesunanin Vanaudicht, Neesthahe ichjeva nau vedaw, Nau Lesous Christos nesaneeth Heeau Henethrnadauin, Hinesunaun Veden Nauwathaw Jevaneatha, Heinaun isaedaeun Mare; Neaudait nauhauchu Pontus Plat, nenetca nau nejeenenad; Neawised hadau beheeaune; Nasees nanee jagauid hethe deneca; na neejaejisad hesehe hieahin, Nau hutha theokut javees. Javaneatha Vasuna Vanaudicht; Hehethehe hadejaut hadnauchuwideed henadeed nea netcad. Nethauwadanau Vedan Nauwathaw Jevaneatha; Nau vedan nechauhadaeu Hwhau Jevaneatha; Nau

Hatjegochdavanadau wochdaut; Nau hajagohainau gujautdaheid vedunieau; Nau hunadeed jethaujene. Ithawu.

Gloria in Excelsis

Hau-wau-ne-dau-naa Ha-sau-nau-ne-ne he-ja-vaa, nau ve-dau-au-wuu da-na-dau-yau-au, hane-yau-da-na-va-na, he-na-ne-da-nede. Nau-wau-ne-dau-na-ne; nau-wau-au-dau-na-ne, ne-ve-ve-the dau-na-ne, ne-chau-gua-na-va-ne, ne-va-vee-ne-the dau-na-ne-heee na-na-ne-me-ha-va-the hau-chau-gua-he-de, Hau Va-ha da he ne He-ja-va-ne-au-thau, Ha-ja-vaa Ne-nau-chu-wu-de, He-ja-va-ne-au-thau He-ne-sau-nau-ne-de Va-he-nau-da-da.

Hau Va-ha-da-he-ne, Ja-sa-sau He-ja-va-ne-au-thu-sau Chris; Hau Va-ha-da-he-ne He ja-va-ne-au-thau, He-au He-Ja-va-ne-au-thau, He-au Ha-sau-nau-ne-ne.

Na-na-ne-dau-sa-nau-wu wau-chu-de he-na-ne-da-ne-de, je-au-wu-nau-naa. Na-na-ne-ne dau-sa-nau-wu wau-chu-dau-de he-na-ne-da-ne-de, je-au-wu-nau-naa. Na-na-ne-ne dau-sa-nau-wu wau-chu-dau-de he-na-ne-da-ne-de je-jaa-the-de-dau dau-ve-ve-the-dau-na-ne. Na-na-ne-ne dau-the-au-gu-ne he-ja-ve-se. He-ja-va-ne-au-thau Hasau-nau-ne-ne, je-auwu-nau-naa. Ha-nau Na-na-ne-ne naa-ne-sa-he-ne dau-chau-guu-va-dan; Na-na-ne-ne naa-ne-sa-he-ne Dau-va-ha-da-he-he; Na-na-ne-ne na-a-ne-sa-ne, Hau-Chris nau-Va-da-nau-wau-thau-wu, Na-na-ne-ne dau-ja-vaa jauu-the-na-ne ha-dau-chau-gu-a-he-de He-ja-va-ne-au-thau Ha-sau-nau-ne-ne.

He-thau-vaa

Shoshone Vocabulary

all .... oi-oot
after a while .... byn-nat
alone .... bin-dag
arrow/pak .... bag-gan e
axe .... ho-wan ni
another .... and-dar es (andres)
another .... kik o mish
arrive .... pe-tunt
arm .... be yr
shoulder .... nash u unt
across/over/man .... iuch
ashamed .... nas so ah/nash unt
ask .... or riv vi
abuse/tease .... nash shwn sap
abuse/cruel .... gish shiu ant
hurt .... wm mar ra
after me/to come .... nia vin-hank
afternoon/after dinner .... dabbi dig-gam-ma
agency .... niw sogwp
all right .... sora-mak
above .... ba hn
all the time .... oi-yous
another .... kic-o-mish
across .... o-hah-ro
abuse .... ma-mit-tu
afraid .... ma-ree-e-ent
among .... ma-re-ga-of-how
angry .... to-ho-vwk
arrest .... ma-zit-ti-man
aunt .... ne-an-pah-hah

break/strike .... sak-ko-va-wh
bread .... tos-te-cup
bread, baked .... gas-sop
beautiful .... san-na-vwint
basket .... se ah woush
boots .... wah bin namp
bite .... na-goo sho nip
brand .... nug o po, dang gop
before .... gist hi e gan

beaver skin .... em-poo
beer .... shoon dit se pah
belt .... nic
beets .... eng-git-tse-na
bacon .... co sho youpe
breakfast .... perch-co tick a ro
bashful .... nash-u int
beard .... mo atts
brass kettle .... awe wit too
bow .... ho ate
boat .... suck
bring to .... sho gope-ma-yack
bird, small .... ho-cho
bird, large .... gwe na
broom .... tin nor
big .... pe-up/be at che
beads .... tsome
bit, to be .... ne get se en
buck .... bi-vat-zuck
blind .... pol e wit
boil .... eh its
bone .... tson ip
born .... pa han
braid hair .... nar an gush ek
brain .... ko vish
bridge .... po sick
brook .... te ah o guap
bullberry .... enga homp
burn, to .... ma go too
blanket .... nav o eeh
bed, cot .... bdl-gwid-hw-ho
branding iron .... te go po
barrel .... wo-vin-bo aas
bottle .... bah--ough
beaver trap .... han-ny-wun
bridle .... timp-at-zan-e gah
bridle bit .... ah rah
brass wire .... o wa wit
black .... tw hw vit
beautiful .... san nab oon-ie
buffalo .... cootch
buffalo robe .... kootch en empoo
buck skin .... yess im bit

buttons .... tay toom buck ah
moccasins .... pah nampa
badger .... ho nah
big man .... bi ar in appwe
brass tacks .... pat se mun gan ny
butter .... bidge e yupe
brother, elder .... um bab it se
brother, younger .... en dam idg ge
buffalo calf .... tuc wat se
bells .... gow wo ho hoi
beans .... pe hw rah
bear, black .... ag wah
bear, grizzly .... woo ra ag wah
blood .... purp
bite .... git se ah
beyond .... o nung wah
bag .... mo gotes
blue .... tve we bit
bucket .... wid doa
bitter .... mo ats
bridge .... bo suck
boats .... suk i
brand .... gop op
bring .... mei ak

chain .... youn gah ru
cough .... o nip
chew .... mo git so whin
certainly .... hog ges sia
count, to .... marit zay
coffee mill .... tiz ze gue ny
coffee .... cap pay
cartridge .... nah bok
cigarettes .... pam na yak
catch up to .... ma rad zah
candle .... yupe te gup-pe-tor
carry it along .... ma-zah yah
catch .... mah mah me gum mah
cross to .... ma ne tu
cook .... guash up
cheat .... te re koult
chop .... ma wa ka
close, near .... ne tit se
council .... ne wis a ra (?)

corral .... bungo gan
cut.. ma zik ka
comb .... nas sat tea
cold .... id jen
chickens .... oni-gwe nah
cups .... nar ak
calico and cloth .... wan up or quash-o
close the door .... me zut to
chain... tim pe ta moop (cloud-dom-hop)
cooked .... bash-up
corn .... han-ne vit
cakes .... to-so tecup guash up penah
courtship .... nash up
crazy .... am up
cry... yag ut
Cheyennes .... pa kan na vo
chewing gum... san er qua
catch .... mat siah
chain... po he wih ti mook
coffee pot .... cappe nit to
crooked .... kay tu na ant
cinch.. nas sup sima gah
candle .... coo net se ah
corn meal .... han ne vit na o sup
cherries.. to a mam pe
cup .... ah wch
cup, china .... dim be a wo
cracker .... pash sha tos sa ti cup
cards .... no hie
cups .... nah rac
sweet.. pe nah ka munt
chair .... gar re or gair e
chicken ....o nah gwee ah
come .... kim
cover .... wo gyn awch
cut... mat se eah
chief... cop e tah, le gwan i(?)
cough .... on nig gin, onip
comb .... naz sid tw yi
clouds .... to mop
church .... nash wn de ga
certainly .... hag gan niu vin
country .... sho go pe

count .... mar rid zi
cock a gun .... ma moomcun
country, big .... man nunk so gwp
go together .... nun nar ag ar iuch
crazy .... eh wap, aim up
contentment .... nan ga hag aneuch (?)

dance .... nic a ro
day .... tabby
daughter .... em bad e
day after tomorrow .... pi no qya - percn
day before yesterday .... hi e gan kint
dawn .... o hah wan ig gi
deaf .... kay ming en
dead .... de ape
deer .... so gwr hi a
died .... dw i yan
dirt .... sho gup
do .... ma han it
don't mind, disobedient .... kay ne nun ga bidge e
don't tell it .... kay o reo wite
down .... to kent
drink .... mah hev v
dream .... nav oo she ai
drive a nail .... ma ran nic
devil .... tao op
drunk .... a ma a kant
dry .... pash up
dust .... ho coo nate
dinner .... tow gwe tick a ro
dark .... kay na vu e kent
dismount .... way or wah
eat .... dic a ro ma ric(?)
ear .... o nanyk
earring .... nou ka sha mo
eaten enough .... su be gus mar rick
egg .... noi or ho no e
eight .... nah y yot so wit
elk .... bar hi par a
embrace .... ma-gwab
encamp .... eng go novide
enough .... sho ve gash
enumerate .... ma rit z
ermine skin .... pah pidge em bet

eruption .... e ets
evening .... yeak
eye .... pw i
exactly/same .... hi up shu wite

fall .... ba heik
fan .... co bah
farm .... shout to mos sink
far .... na na gwr
fast .... nam ish a
fat .... youp
feather .... se ah
fell .... ma mas oon gan
feet .... namp
fight, bull .... nav id yn gin
fingers .... mo sho wie
fingernail.. mo ahe to
fire .... wai ant
find .... may row rah
fish .... bek we
five .... man ah git
fit .... to gw it
flag .... wan up pa tan ze yah kant
flat .... se a pa-gant
Flatheads .... to ta se van ne
flour .... to sho te cup
fly .... an e boo ic
foot .... fo quash o ganie
Frenchman .... U an ti bo
fruit .... bo compi
friend .... hansh
forget .... ma nash u wad se
fox, black .... to wan
fox, red .... on to wan ny
full ....dip u gan
friend .... shih mas na hansh
funeral .... mar rig gie guon do
funny .... nan as snom sum mite
fragrance .... san-gwan ar

gallop .... im meah
girl.. ni ve or im bed e
give me ....ma ut
give me horse ....na vongu mik

glass, looking .... nav voo
gloves .... mapa sook
goes with .... o rag a van
go to .... me ar ro
go fast.. git tan nook
going to town ....pah emert
good.. sant
good smell .... zant gua nah
grass, green .... poo ip
grass, dry .... shaw nip
grasshopper ....ah tunk
grey .... ash am bit
green backs .... wan na boy e wih
grey head.. tos sa wit pam be get
grease wood.. tow mo pe
guess.. to swn na gish
grieve.. dwt ha nia shwn gar
gun .... pe ate
gun hammer .... a te an wak
go.. nook
go and get it .... nuk me ak
ghost .... tso op
green .... segip-evooe-vit
hair.. pam be kant
halter .... te he gar eh
hand ....um moo ah
half .... sing we uo nun gua
half-breed .... tibosin gue get
half .... sing wipe
hard .... git ant
handle or bail .... ma nat zoo ya
happiness .... sa nea shoon gan
hang ....tsa wei
happy..san nia shwn gar or sant nash shoon gar
hare .... to sho cam
hat ....diz zong mo i
hay .... shaw nip
handkerchief .... wanaga rook
help .... ne re ma zom mo
heard ....mo mungen
heavy .... pwe tent
heaven .... dw gwm ban ag
heart .... be mem pe(?)

herd .... ma ric co on
here .... sick or ig-ish
hide .... wads issue or waz zi teg
high .... pant or ba ent
hiccough .... hen nin
hired man .... tier re oup
headache .... pam pe nid zie gua
hog .... co sho
hobbles .... bungo mo wit tah mah
hook .... naz zwn
hold .... man zike
home .... yn gan i
honest .... kay ish um
horn of a saddle .... o aah
horse .... bungo
horse, lost .... ne am bungo wazin
horse, back .... to he gar eh
house .... gan
hungry .... pah du ah
hunt .... ma wic
hunting for game .... te ya guanto

island .... ba moo sa shan din
Indian .... nim-ah
ice .... pah cup
inside .... man dike ko punt
idleness .... ha-hima hanid gin(?)

jellies .... pe nah gum ba
joking .... nar ish shwn hak
jump .... paw pe do
jointy .... denes hoon gantyanna(?)

kill .... mah vic, wig-gar-ro(?)
keep or put away .... ma rig gie
knee .... un ta an up
knife .... hab be weeh
knock .... rod di go i gint

lamp .... te gup pe tor
lame .... pe ti wit
lake .... pah kah re
last summer .... moon nan hua
laugh .... yan a kin
lead to .... ma zank

legs .... oom
leggings .... o ma wit tah ma
leaf... boo ip
limp .... pi to hwet
lift .... ar riv i ah
lift ....ma za yeh
lice .... po se ia
lie, untruth .... ish amp
listen .... mo nun ga he
light pail ....u nit tit se
little .... dea-dit-se
lightening .... toom yac ah
lock the door .... git tah ma zuk to
love .... nash um
long time dead .... n zo op
lose .... ooi pan
lock .... ma-dzid-it
lie down... hobe
lie to .... ish an ei
like to .... ga mung gun or zant nash un gan
legend .... nar-re-gu-guh

marsh .... seg-we-dant
make .... ma han
man .... dun ap pwe
many.. shont
married.. peroh an gwe kent
marry a woman .... a gwea to ro
marry a man .... con ma ru ru
matches .... ho gos op
meal .... han neep
me .... ne ah
meet .... we gi am
Mexican .... to yo ri bo
mean.. kag shoo unt
metals ....tin pe
medicine... nat a so
medicine man.. bo ho gant
midnight.. to gua to gan
mid summer ....tog gwe taots
mid winter .... tog gwe to omp
mine ....ne a himp
mink .... bam bo ka
middle .... un ach

milk .... be ji
mix .... nak ka va oi agus ma hanna
money, silver .... timpe bw ea wit
moose .... to par ie
mouse trap .... pampo ny wum
more .... twish
money .... poo e wit
month .... sum mw mu ia
morning .... be etch chws or pen che co
moon .... mu ia
moccasin .... namp
mosquito .... mo po us
mount .... te ya a ro i can
mud .... se gwip
mountain .... to yap-doi-ab bi (toe-yo)(?)
mouse .... bam boo na
mouth .... timp
mule .... moo lah
muskrat .... bam bo ka

naughty .... ka shu unt
needles .... wan na weet
night .... to gan
now .... eg git se
none .... kay wut
noon .... tog gwe tabby
nose bleed .... mo vin doo taan
north fork .... sho o gwap

odor .... a gwon ah
old man or anything .... so go put see
old woman .... hiv ve zot sie
one .... sim it se
onion .... kink
one year old .... tum in dwa
open the door .... ma zut to wah
on top .... ov up
otter .... pan zook
over .... o nah
overshoes .... tuck a namp
outside .... hom pe nun gua
our .... dam
often .... son na
office .... deu-o-gan

paint .... bish up
paper .... tib oop
Paint Rock .... Tim pe tan na vo og wap
pasture .... shon ne taz wop May pass mia mi; nas un de hei (?)
pepper .... to o na bit
plant .... tim as see in kin do
people .... shont a neer
picture .... ne win na rope
pinto .... ash in av it
pipe .... toke or to we
pines .... wo ong go pi
plains .... pa wit se
pins .... pum pa we or bam bi wi hw
plough .... to gon mie
pocket .... en te mo gotes
porcupine .... yi ir
play .... nw hint(?)
powder .... nag gots
potatoes .... tz i na
poor .... tit a nah kant
prairie dog .... tind say
proud .... na van ah vite
put on your clothes .... ma ma sook
put it there .... ik marik
pants .... peet sook
purple .... aqui vit
put up a tent .... gan ni ha
plume .... dotse hi gan
pleasant .... sa(?)

quick .... gita or nam a soo
quirt .... nip pa

rabbit .... tap(b?) oot se
ran .... na na area o
rat .... ye a vit sie
rain .... pah a mar
rainbow .... pah o gwo a bit
red .... ank a bit
rest .... gwia-man
recover .... que cho nah or guid-djw-i(?)
rice .... war te cup
ring .... man e gar
rock .... timp

reins .... nar ri muk
roll .... ma woot a
road .... bo
rosebush .... tsi up
round .... toom bo nate
rub .... nash oi ip
river .... og-wip(?)

Saturday .... da-mu-ip-pa
salt .... o na bit or toso-o-nap
saddle .... nar rino
sage chickens .... po ho gin nah
sack .... mog otes
sagebrush(?)
Sage Creek .... Po ho og wa
saw .... ho zik kah
scabs .... te man i kah
say .... tay gwe na
shawl .... nus a ge
shake hands .... mo od dsai
scratch .... do dsa so y wch
shovel .... sho go ho rup
short .... ku ba dit se
shot .... ma goat
sheep, mountain .... mu zam bi e
sheep skin .... toke em poo
sheepeaters .... toke o re ka
shirt .... quash o
sheep .... gar ri wkw
shoulder .... ne zo ungo
shut .... mat sat to
shoes .... namp
ship .... peah such
see .... bu wick
shot .... week
school .... de wop we gan
scissors .... dig go ap
sick .... nid dzi guar
sinue .... iwn dam
Sioux .... Pam pidg e mun e or pam piz e meah
sign talk .... ma wo ya guin
sleep .... ep wi
snake .... togo a
sneeze .... ah gwo skin

```
sneak off ................................................................ wadze meah
seed ...................................................... te mah se en gah
small pox .............................................................. ta as sie
speak loud ...................................................... pe an go rake
skin .......................................................................... peg up
snow .................................................................. tuck ah vit
sharp .................................................................... kamup
smell ...................................................................... mah eke
steal ...................................................................... ma rid ic
starved to death ................................................ con e de ape
strong .................................................................... git tant
strawberries .................................................. an ga po kam be
strychnine ...................................................tsh up pa ma nab su
stove .................................................................. te kot to
stone .......................................................................... tim by
store .............................................................. mar e ma kan
stomach ...................................................................... supp
straight ................................................................tu na ant
seed ...................................................... te mah se en gah
soft ...................................................................... u ni tet se
supper .............................................................. ye tick aro
spit ........................................................................ tos sin
stirrup .............................................................. nar a tig gy
sing ..................................................................di-nig-huant
stop ........................................................................ kish
spoon .............................................................. tay goo yah
Sunday .............................................................. Pi ar rab bi
smoke .................................................................... gwi ket
strike .................................................................... wit two
springs ..........................................................ba ris sop pa
stumble .......................................................... mwr rig ga
sky, clear ...................................................... toot za wit
sugar ...................................................................... pee nah
soap .................................................................... te go sho
sour ..........................................................sig ging go muk
steamboat ......................................................gwna saki
swollen .................................................................. be gwa
sweet................................................................ pe-nah-munt
sundance ......................................................dag-oo-wan-na
tall ........................................................................ giw vir ant
talk ....................................................................ta guin
take ...................................................................... mi yak
tea ...................................................................... poo ie ha
```

tear .... mat sash i
teeth .... dam mu
tent .... wana gan ny
that .... sook
thread .... wan ar rap
thus .... soo wite
trade .... ma re mere o
trap .... wan ny
trail .... bo he
there .... sook
take it .... mee ak
tobacco .... bam
tired .... ba ho wy gan
thunder .... toom yac cah
turn .... co i i
today .... tab by
thigh .... bing up
truth .... te bits
thick .... po hun dent
thirsty .... da gwt tie
telescope .... tib boo whe h
tongue .... e kw
throat .... gw itsh

unlock .... mat ze too
understand .... shum banah(?)
untie .... ma roy ah
ugly .... te chy
unsuitable .... kay mah shome pe sup
Utes .... Ute a
under clothing .... to ki e quash o
undecided .... tish u wan sip

very .... teeb it se
vest .... a mat zan e gah

wash .... mah gwoot cheu
water .... pah
weazle .... pam pidg e
well .... paysh en sant
what .... hagan
weigh .... ma man aka
white man .... tibo
want .... ma soo int
whiskers .... mates

wind .... toomp
whip .... ni yp ai
whistle .... coo sha tin e guon
willow .... she her bit
wind .... ne ate
woman .... wipe
white .... to sho bit
wood stick .... hwp-gwan
worm .... wo ab bi
weep .... yag ah
wolf .... t djap u
who .... hagar
wrap .... ma gwand dwi
work .... dir ah i

yawn .... it tam mar
you .... nim
yes .... hah
yesterday .... kint
yellow .... o ah bit

Shoshone Phrases

sweep the floor .... du no a
wash the dishes .... a w go idjo
game with arrows ....nash e an
skin scraper .... tes eep
to rub a skin .... sunk o nash o cant
thick furred .... sho ho pah e gant
whose lodge is this .... tish hock en gan ne
tell him to come .... ma ra ru
light a fire .... ma gut o
are you sick .... yn ha nidzik
are you better... yn ha san na hun
give me ....na ut
hive him ....ma ut
give me a horse .... na vongu mak
give me some money...................................... na bu i ui mak
give them .... ma ri ut
fetch rations ....na mu ipe iak
put it here .... hik mar ik
go and get it .... nuk meak
did you hear .... yn ha an gach
I heard him .... nea suk anangach
when will you come .... in himba gim hond

I want some water .... oa its sue
please give me some water .... na va ium
i am thirsty .... ne ra gud de ix
lead your horse .... im bunk sang ak u
lead my horses .... im oung ne sang ak unx
I have lost my horse .... nea ratz na vong ne wad zi
I will hunt him up .... nia ro ur ri uig
I will speak to her .... nia ma ma an deg aro
ask her .... ma ruv ve
day before yesterday .... hei e gana go
come to church .... dan nash sund de ha doichat gim
I sleep .... nia abwich
I did not sleep .... ne a ga ep wi
church/prayer house .... nash wn de gar
Son of god .... Dam Appwe un dwa
What is your name .... haga yn naniak
I see .... nia a awik
you see .... yn awik
it's warm .... euant
he is fat .... id e up
he is thin .... id eng gan a vits
in the woods ....soho gav
a hillside.. no havedin sa vech
where flowers grow .... booip seagan
among pine trees .... woon go vit seagan
maple trees .... bena hoopseagan
place to rest .... ish pin ga yoont
place to eat ....ish bing a yooint yn dig a
where berries grow .... se bo hoom segan
under blue skies .... doo goon did sa wit
on the shore........................... bea va un gu math ogwie un gunach(?)
among trees .... hoop in gav
a good house .... san un gan
our home .... dam ungan
it is enough .... sov ve gesh
a fishing place .... dam be ngua gar
a hunting place .... dam dehoowe gar
when two roads cross .... bo we wa ra gaw(?)
where the family meets .... dan un gan gar buk na wa
when the winds blow ....bunchan oo naar(?)
house with many rooms .... gan ne so dar a want
eagle nest .... gwana ungan
long view man .... ank e vooik(?)
a shady place .... hig e a chant

a high place .... bahint
a rocky place .... sont din he gant
in the meadow .... shoshoni daint
where birds sing .... hoo joo un dinooe gar
looking toward sunset .... dabe you ic megar booit
looking toward sunrise .... dabe un do ik a vooik
summer camp .... dats un gan
on the road .... bo oit
overlooking the .... ba ogooip a vooit
in the orchard .... bo gombe hoop
when friends meet .... dan hanch na wagar
a peaceful place .... sant so gop
valley .... se e pa gant
far off .... man angwar(?)
big water .... bea ba
many birds .... shont hoojoo
many boats .... shont sak
mutual love .... san as oon gant
a little hill .... dea nove
by the brook .... ba un gu mach
by the spring .... ba ris opa un gumach
on the cliff .... dim ba nach

Shoshone Relations

mother .... am bea
father .... ap wa
in-law .... nea ma do go
wife .... ma gwo pa
husband .... en go ma pa
aunt .... bah ah
nephew .... ar rah
niece .... bahah
mother's father .... do go
father's father .... gyn noo
father's mother .... hood see
wife's father .... nim do go
husband's father .... nim mus gyn noo
wife's mother .... nim mun gag oo
mother-in-law .... ne a ma go go
brother-in-law .... da itch
son-in-law .... moon up pa
sister-in-law .... mea...(?)
sister, elder .... bad ze
young sister .... mam me

young brother .... dam me
grand child .... un do go
grandmother.. ga i go
grandfather .... toh gah

Shoshone Animals

antelope .... quaritz
antelope buck .... wantz
antelope skin .... quar em poo e
bear .... warrah
grizzly .... tosa wurrah
brown bear .... outa wurrah
yellow bear .... oa wurrah agwa
black bear .... doo wurrah
beaver .... hav ne
bobcat .... me am be or se rook goc
bald eagle .... bas sea
buck deer .... doo tea
female deer .... so go rea un doo a
cranc .... wass
coyote .... teah ish a pa
sand crane .... hillgo an dat ta
crow .... kak/gak
dog.. sar re
geese .... ne gint
horse .... de he
lynx .... doo goo vitch
mink .... doo bas we bas saw
mountain lion... do ya roo goo
muskrat .... bam bw ka
mallard .... boo ye
mole... do mo wit o gwa
salmon .... a gae
sparrow/hawk .... ge ne
skunk .... bo ne ats
squirrel .... woon go rats
red fox .... enga wd ne
seal(?) .... si e(?)
elk.. bar re
jay .... wo yw a de a
trout .... sa ben gwe
turtle .... bea yag wad sa

Shoshone Places

Crowheart Butte .... Ha i am b he
Dry Creek .... po gp no og wap
Washakie Needles .... Boo it te oonna
Owl Creek .... Mo am bitch
South Fork Canyon ....Tim bannagov
Agency .... Niu so gup
Bull Lake .... Pah gwe che yah gah
Big Horn Mountains .... Tum bo a to yap

Shoshone Numbers

one .... sim me
two .... wad dw
three .... ba et
four .... wad zw it
five .... man i git
six .... na ha vat
seven .... dad zw it
eight .... ni a wadzw wit
nine ....
ten .... si a more
eleven .... sim ma undo ing int
twelve .... wad dw
thirteen .... ba et
twenty .... wam rar
twenty-one .... wa i mor simma undo ing
thirty .... ba him or
thirty-one.. ba him simma undoi
forty .... wadz wi sim o wr
fifty .... managis simor
sixty .... nav az simor
seventy .... dadzwe simor
eighty .... nia wadz wi simore
ninety .... sim mar win
one hundred .... sim me mos simor
one hundred fifty .... sim me managis mando igi
two hundred .... wadw mos somm

Acknowledgments

Thank you

To my grandfather, who chose to spend his life with the Indians, teaching and helping them to cope in the new white world.

To my mother, who spent many years of her life going over my grandfather's papers and notes and composing a rough draft of the book.

To my husband, who spent many hours waiting for me to research and copy just a few more pages of notes and papers that I found!

To Patty Trautman, who read my book and realized that it had historical value, and decided, with my permission, to do something about it now!

To Sharon Kahin, who read my papers and notes at the University of Wyoming Library, then applied for and received a grant to be used to arrange the original notes, and to edit my manuscript.

I will give myself credit for never doubting that I had a book of much historical value.

To my friends who gave so much to the final printing of the book and their faith in me, and their interest in the historical background of our friends and neighbors, the Shoshone and Arapahoe people.

To Roslyn Westman, our typist and critic, for long days and weekends.

To the donors who contributed resources to this project:

Jim and Alice Marie Guschewsky
Guy Lytle of Sewanee, Tennessee
Jack and Alice Nicholas
Dave and Mae Raynolds and Lander Pioneer Museum
Harry and Alex Tipton
Garry and Pat Trautman
Mike and Mary Young (Mary is the great-granddaughter of J. Roberts)

Beatrice Crofts, 1997